Your Roadmap to
Retirement Riches

Your Roadmap to
Retirement Riches
(so you don't have to work
in your old age)

Steven Yamshon, CFS® CMFC®

INVESTMENT COUNSELOR,
STEVENS FIRST PRINCIPLES INVESTMENT ADVISORS
FORMER VISITING SCHOLAR AND FACULTY,
ANDERSON GRADUATE SCHOOL OF MANAGEMENT AT UCLA
LECTURER, UNIVERSITY OF CALIFORNIA, LOS ANGELES

Literary Press
Newport Beach, CA
www.literarypress.com

Library of Congress Control Number: 2004099082
ISBN 0-9716958-9-X

Printed in the United States of America

To Adriana
who makes my life worth living
and who has changed my perspective
on life and the world.

Contents

Acknowledgments

Thanks to **Robert Woodcox,** my editor, for his support
and terrific editing skills during the writing of this book. I
would also like to thank Professor Moshe Rubinstein of UCLA
who has always encouraged me to write a simple book for those
who need some straightforward investment direction. To my
present and past UCLA students who continue to make my
teaching efforts worthwhile and enjoyable.

Although Benjamin Graham and Murray Rothbard have
passed away, I am indebted to these towering figures of
finance and economics. Without their teachings and writing I
would not have received the keys to financial wisdom and success.

Foreword

The unique feature of *Your Roadmap to Retirement Riches* is its very purpose—to provide the general public, in small measure, with the kind of service Steven Yamshon has been providing family, friends, and clients. It is a service characterized by the highest levels of dedication, loyalty, personal integrity, professional competence and excellence. This book is the result of pursuing this noble purpose to be of service to the general public of potential investors. It is a simple, easy to read guide to help match personality traits with compatible prudent investment strategies.

The book distills years of teaching, research, and professional practice in the field of investments. Steven Yamshon devoted three years of his career as a visiting scholar at UCLA Anderson School of Management. During that period he performed in-depth research in pursuit of core ideas and guiding principles for prudent strategies for investing. In the years that followed he continued to refine his ideas by presenting them in his popular university courses and seminars. Concurrently with the teaching and research, the ideas underwent the crucial tests in the marketplace. Steven initially tested the ideas by taking personal risk before he deployed them with clients. His company, Steven's First Principles Investment Advisors, has had a remarkable record of investment success using Steven's tested strategies.

For greatest benefit from the book, it is advisable to follow these steps. First, read the book. Follow the advice of what to avoid. Then, study the book to find the strategy that is suitable for you, and finally, embrace Your Roadmap to Retirement Riches to implement the strategy of your choice. These steps constitute a prudent strategy to invest your time for the purpose of achieving a prosperous future with no regrets.

— Moshe F. Rubinstein
Professor, UCLA
Los Angeles, California
October 2004

Preface

Before beginning my career as an investment advisor, I was a Security Analyst, a job I enjoyed. It was my responsibility to read company annual reports and try to decipher their finances— always a challenge, but also fun. It also provided valuable information for my firm's clients, which gave me a great deal of satisfaction. Since that first job, I have analyzed thousands of companies and made many people rich, or at least made them a great deal of money.

When I started my own investment-counseling firm, I found that clients wanted something more than just asset management — they wanted sound advice and counseling as well. They expected me to continue to select stocks and bonds, but they were also concerned about their retirements, diversification, and other issues, so they often asked for my advice in these matters.

These needs prompted me to strive for a greater level of ongoing education in many areas, more than I'd needed as a Security Analyst. I found that I enjoyed the learning process as much as the application of that knowledge.

Two investment topics of major concern that have evolved from my practice and my studies are *diversification* and *retirement*. I find that these two subjects are the most important to the investors I work with, probably because these are the two that they know the least about.

If you're like most of my clients, you prefer simplicity to complexity, particularly when it comes to an investment plan. However, many investors often get duped into following a complicated roadmap, for a variety of reasons, and this is not only unfortunate, but most assuredly, unnecessary.

When I was a Visiting Scholar at the Anderson Graduate School of Management at UCLA, I was determined to find the Holy Grail of investing. Since I'd already studied Benjamin Graham's investing philosophy in detail, his ideas were a natural place for me to start, so I wrote to Graham's most famous pupil, Warren Buffett, and I asked if I could visit him, with the thought that perhaps he would help me in my quest.

To my surprise, he actually wrote back saying that Graham's ideas were lucid, simple, and readily available — in effect saying, "You don't need my help."

Graham's ideas all center on simplicity, from concepts to implementation. However, even though he never did actually find the "perfect" simple system, he was right in espousing it because, as you will discover as you read this book, successful investing really isn't difficult. In fact, it's quite simple.

A couple of years ago, I was having dinner with a friend who is a municipal finance expert, and shortly after our entrees were served, our conversation turned to the stock market.

He told me, despite his financial background (which was considerable), that he had NEVER been successful picking stocks, though he struggled with it for more than 40 years.

I was dumbfounded. I couldn't believe what he'd said. After relating many of the mistakes he'd made over the years, I told him that if he stuck to a simple, long-term plan, his success would certainly improve, at least 1000%.

Picking stocks and bonds is difficult for many people because it involves psychology, not just financial research. Then, of course, there is the "emotional" element, which can be fatal. The late Benjamin Graham wrote in the *Intelligent Investor* that the investor's chief problem, and even his worst enemy, is likely to be himself. I've thought many times how often that is true in the multitudes of investors.

Instead of thinking forward 10 years or more (depending upon their age), many people panic when their selections go down in a month. The Internet has only exacerbated this emotionalism, allowing investors to check their portfolios, day-by-day, or even minute-by-minute.

Yes, analyzing stocks has become more complex, but investing hasn't.

In this book, I will provide you with some of the techniques you can use to simplify and enhance your investments, and will illustrate why it is so important to save and to diversify.

Will the typical investor normally beat the market benchmarks by a wide margin? No, because in order to beat those benchmarks, the average investor would have to spend an inordinate amount of time studying securities, something most people do not have the time or even patience for — in fact, most professional money managers can't even beat the benchmarks.

This book will give you the information you need to improve your investment choices and performance, through diversification and saving.

Please enjoy.
Steve Yamshon

Introduction
You need money to retire on and you can't
depend on Uncle Sam.

As you are undoubtedly aware, the world of investing
has become extremely complex with a bewildering array
of choices, and it only looks as though it will get worse.

Unfortunately, the majority of investments ultimately turn out to be losers.
Many investors, after years of stock market
gains and then large losses, have also lost
their confidence, particularly in recent years
as a result of the dot com bust.

> **"One faces the
> future with
> one's past."**
> –Pearl S. Buck.
> "China Faces the
> Future" lecture,
> New York City, 13
> October 1942

Investors fail more often than not,
because they don't follow some basic rules
of investing. Now that they are faced with
retirement, many are finding they don't
have enough funds and will have to reduce their standards of
living-in many cases, drastically.

Though ordinary citizens make more money now than 10
years ago, they are finding that it buys less and less.

"Health costs rising faster than incomes, study says,"
barked a recent *USA Today* article. The story by William
Welch went on to say," Health insurance paid by U.S. workers
has risen nearly three times faster than the average earnings in
the past four years, eroding the income of average Americans,
according to a study based on federal data.

"Premium costs for private health insurance coverage grew 35.9% from 2000 to 2004. Average individual earnings grew 12.4%, the study found."

"As health premiums consume a growing share of earnings, more Americans are spending a major portion of their annual incomes on health care."

And health care is just one of many inflationary activities that is eroding your buying power, not to mention your savings.

Another emotional facet of an individual's finances involves debt. Many people feel richer than they are because they are able to purchase far more than they have the actual cash or savings to pay for. They go deeper and deeper into debt and eventually find out they aren't really worth what they thought they were. Often times, they're in denial about their debts.

If you add the ravages of inflation to debt, all of a sudden, the average person finds out he no longer has what he needs to make it through his or her retirement years. If you add unscrupulous brokers and financial advisors who enrich themselves at the cost of hurting their own clients well...you've all seen the stories of men and women in the late fifties going to work at Home Depot or Wal-Mart, to make ends meet-a sad state of affairs indeed. Unfortunately, that is an example of retiring dumb.

Consider this book a toolbox that will give you, even if you only have moderate resources, instruments you need to build and maintain a strong capital base. If you aren't "rich" and only have moderate resources, know this-you will have to save more and spend less. It's just that simple.

According to Alan Greenspan in his testimony to Congress recently, unless the government acts quickly, there won't be enough funds in the Social Security system to fully fund all the benefits that we have been promised. This was his fourth warning on the subject, but those in Congress are more interested in being re-elected, than they are worrying about your retirement. If you think I'm wrong, consider this: Congressmen and Senators do not contribute to the

Social Security system, so they do not have the same interests as you. They don't have to worry if the system fails,
because they have their own very, very generous plans-all
paid for by you, the taxpayer. It's called the Congressional
and Executive Branch Retirement Plan. Consider this: In the
2004 election year for President of the United States,
President George Bush and Senator John Kerry didn't even
debate or discuss the looming bankruptcy of Social Security
and plan how to avoid it.

Greenspan went on to say that there is NO possibility that
the benefits currently promised could be delivered and he further put everyone on notice that they had better start saving
more now!

Not Saving Enough

Sadly, most Americans spend more than they make, which
leaves little or no room for savings. Even the rich often spend
more than they make. The simple key then is not only to begin
saving more, but also to diversify whatever you are saving and
then invest in a smart way.

In the August, 2004 issue of *Barons*, Randall Forsyth reported that 4 in 10 workers are not saving enough for retirement.
After the 2000 market decline, many retirees were invested in
speculative stocks, hoping to win the lottery and because of
the decline; many of them were wiped out. In addition, of
course, the scandals that rocked Wall Street and continue to
do so, didn't help either.

There are two types of speculators: Those who have lost and those who are going to lose.

Robert Schiller, the Yale Economist, who wrote the best selling
book, *Irrational Exuberance*, recently conducted a survey in
which the respondents believed that home prices would continue to increase by 20% or more during this coming decade.

Electricians, plumbers and other contractors rushed in and began leveraging themselves into homes and then "flipping" them (buying and selling quickly using borrowed money), in an effort to get rich quick.

I know one such couple that knew nothing about real estate and had no experience in investing in it, with the exception of their own home. They're now buying homes in Phoenix, Arizona hoping to make a quick buck *flipping* them.

This is the same mentality we saw in the stock market of the 1990s, when the average investor began speculating in something he and she knew nothing about. At the time of this writing (mid 2004), technology and Internet stocks have lost more than 60% of their value, so many of those who speculated in these investments are now turning to real estate.

As an investment advisor, I, of course, see my client's financial lives intimately and for many of them, the picture is bleak. Most will have to reduce their lifestyles in retirement because they have not saved enough and have spent too much.

As an educator (I teach at UCLA), I know that the majority of people don't even have a basic knowledge of personal finance. At a Harvard seminar on Behavioral Finance in the fall of 2003, a professor told the audience that recent studies had suggested that a full 95% of the population did not understand simple financial matters.

In his testimony to Congress in the spring of 2004, Alan Greenspan told the committee that the average American didn't even possess the financial knowledge taught in high school.

I predict that the finances of the average American household will continue to worsen when you couple their lack of understanding with inflation. Only time will prove me right.

The objective of this book is not to turn you into a securities expert or even how to get rich quick. The purpose is to provide you with a simple way to increase and manage your wealth and then to hang onto that which you have accumulated. If you don't learn and apply these simple concepts, you will eventually be on your own. Do you want to become a clerk at Wal-Mart when you're 62?

Let's get started...

The Virtue of Saving
The need to save more and spend less

Bill worked all his life as an advertising executive. He worked right up until he was 65, not an unusual occurrence in his field. In his peak years, he was earning more than $200,000 a year, and he lived an extravagant lifestyle to match his income. He owned expensive cars, frequently dined out at fine restaurants with his wife and friends, and traveled to exotic locales on an annual basis.

> **"Pack your own parachute."**
> –T.L. Hakala

Bill and his wife had two children, but they were grown up and on their own. When Bill turned 65, he had saved approximately $500,000 and had $2,000,000 worth of equity in his home. He had no other assets, nor did he have a pension (not unlike many Americans).

Through Social Security, Bill will receive $27,516 a year. In order for him to maintain his lifestyle, he'll need approximately $5,000,000 in invested assets if he wants to live nicely for another 25 years, and then be able to leave some of his estate to his younger wife and his children.

It's clear that Bill is in trouble. Because he doesn't have enough assets to support his lifestyle, he will have to drastically change the way he lives — now — in order to make ends meet.

So, what about those people who have even less, or who only have moderate means or don't have $2,000,000 in equity in their homes? (And these days, $2,000,000 in equity, does *not* mean what it used to!) According to the *Los Angeles Times*, the average cost of a home in Newport Beach, California, is well over $1 million, and that's the *average*. Even in Riverside and San Bernardino Counties in California (areas that are much less affluent), homes are selling for $400,000 to $500,000!

Another client of mine — with approximately $26,000,000 in assets — retired at the age of 49. When he did, I told him and his wife that they should keep their spending limited to $800,000 a year. Because they aren't following my advice but, instead, are spending much more than I recommended, I've told them that I project they will run out of money by the time he is 70. If he's only planning to live that long, fine — if not, will he be the first 70-year old fast food restaurant cashier?

I brought up these two examples to demonstrate that it doesn't matter how much money you have; if you don't spend within your limits, you're doomed. If they want to live a super rich life into their 80s and 90s, even the super rich need to think about retirement planning.

In order to retire comfortably, many financial planners state that a person needs approximately 80% of what his or her average income was before retirement. My experience has shown that this figure is closer to 100% of what a person earned — especially new retirees who have a tendency to spend more freely after they quit work. They want to travel, eat well, be entertained and pampered, and enjoy the fruits of their long years of labor. As reality quickly sets in, they begin to recognize the warning signs and have a tendency to slow things down a bit.

The fact is: most people don't spend 20% less after they retire. In fact, they spend the same — if not more — than they did prior to retiring.

Like Alan Greenspan, politicians have known about funding gaps for many years, but they are unwilling to correct the problem. Why? Being reelected means promising more and more to constituents. The problem is that, with the exception of raising taxes, there are no other new revenue sources — which isn't even popular with Democrats in an election year.

How long will your money last?

Financial Planner Deena Katz, in her book *Taking Charge of Your Retirement*, has developed a table that projects how long your money will last based on different rates of return (see Figure 1).

Figure 1
How Long the Money Will Last (in years)

Withdrawal	Rate of Return											
	1%	2%	3%	4%	5%	6%	7%	8%	9%	10%	11%	12%
12%	7	8	8	8	8	9	9	10	10	11	12	13
11%	8	8	9	9	9	10	10	11	12	13	14	15
10%	9	9	10	10	10	11	12	13	14	15	17	19
9%	10	10	11	11	12	13	14	15	16	18	21	26
8%	11	11	12	13	14	15	16	18	20	24	30	*
7%	12	13	14	15	16	18	20	22	27	36	*	*
6%	14	15	16	18	19	22	23	31	44	*	*	
5%	17	18	20	22	24	29	36	*	*	*		
4%	20	22	25	28	33	42	*	*	*			
3%	25	28	33	39	*	*	*	*				
2%	35	40	50	*	*	*	*					
1%	*	*	*	*	*	*						

Source: Deena Katz

If you believe, as I do, that the average rate of return on your investments will be 6% to 8% over the next decade (2004-2014), then we can look at Figure 1 to determine how long our assets will last. For this example, let us assume that the rate of return is 6% and your rate of withdrawal is 4%. Your money should last 42 years. By using Figure 1, you can project different scenarios using various rates of returns and withdrawals. In planning, I always use a conservative 6% rate of return and a withdrawal rate of between 4% and 5%. If your assets return more than 6%, that's great, but it is best to plan on the conservative side. For example, if a person has $3,000,000 in assets, using a 6% return and a 4% withdrawal rate, he can safely draw $120,000 per year.

If you have retirement income from sources other than your liquid funds (e.g., rental property income or defined benefit retirement plans), the withdrawal rate you will need from your invested assets to fund your retirement will be less.

Prepare a Balance Sheet

To figure out how much money you will need to draw from your asset base your first step should be to prepare a balance sheet as shown in Figure 2 below. This will tell you how large your asset base needs to be. I have drafted a simplified sample balance sheet that anyone can use.

Figure 2
Model Balance Sheet

Liquid Assets

Checking	$29,000
Money Markets	$50,000
IRA	$200,000
Domestic Equities	$300,000
International Equities	$50,000
REITS	$50,000
TIPS	$100,000
US Treasuries	$100,000
Gold	$21,000
Municipal Bonds	$100,000
Total Liquid Assets	**$1,000,000**

Fixed Assets

Residence	$560,000
Car	$15,000
Total Fixed Assets	**$575,000**

Liabilities

Residential Mortgage	$420,000
Car Loan	$20,000
Total Liabilities	**$440,000**

Net Worth	**$1,135,000**

In Figure 2, the investor has a net worth of $1,135,000. However, $575,000 of this amount is invested in his home and car and should not be included as part of his asset base calculations for retirement planning, unless he plans to sell his homes and downsize or rent.

The proper figure for retirement planning purposes is $1,000,000. Based on this figure, the retiree can withdraw 4% of $1,000,000, or $40,000 per year. You see $1,000,000 doesn't go very far in today's dollar. Think about what $1,000,000 will be worth in the future. It is better to start saving and prepare today so you will have enough money to retire on. Except for his IRA, this investor broke down the various categories of assets properly. Separate your liquid assets from you fixed assets in your balance sheet. Your house, if needed, may produce some retirement funds through a reverse mortgage.

Most of us cannot count on Social Security, and that's a fact. In planning for my clients' retirements, I always use a conservative rate of return, which I firmly believe to be in my clients' interests. In addition to your planning, always remember to consider the erosion factor of inflation. It will never go away.

Many Web sites will help you calculate how much you need to save for retirement, or to determine how long your savings will last. I have some financial calculators on my Web site — **www.stevensfirstprinciples.com** — that I invite you to use. You can also go to **www.yahoo.com** and **www.fp.edu** for this kind of information.

The *Wall Street Journal* recently reported that there is also a good calculator called "The Retirement Probability Analyzer," which is available from The Society of Actuaries Web site at **www.soa.org**. Follow the directions carefully, but if you have multiple sources of income, it may provide you with only limited use.

For you to figure out how many years your money will last, you will need to estimate how long you will live past the date you quit working. Actuarial tables give us this information as well. As an example, a man retiring at age 65 might live to be 85. However, if his spouse is 45 years old, then the number of years the money will last will have to be longer, perhaps 50 years.

Whatever you use to calculate your money's longevity, use the age of the youngest spouse or beneficiary.

To use these charts and some of the other tools that I will be giving you, you need to prepare a personal balance sheet first and keep track of your expenses. Your household budget is an excellent place to begin. You can use Microsoft's Money program, a simple spreadsheet, or a pad and pencil — whatever suits you best. But, first, to determine what you'll need for retirement, you have to know what it's costing you to live (see, I told you this was all simple!).

Keep Track of How Much You Spend

Like keeping strict count of calories when you're dieting, guessing at your expenses isn't something to be taken lightly. Besides, when you write them ALL down, it really forces you to think about where you're spending your money and if you're spending it wisely.

When I first starting disciplining myself to do this (it wasn't easy for me either), I cringed at some of the things I bought during the week, and it wasn't long before I thought twice before spending my money frivolously.

My friend Jerry used to make fun of me in front of our mutual friends because I kept track of all my expenses. I needed a roadmap to see where I was going and the way to provide that is to have a record of what you spend, which is the beginning of how to make sound financial decisions.

Every person and household should develop a personal balance sheet and income statement, which will help you to determine how much money you will need to have as your base.

A personal balance sheet reflects your financial position at any given point in time. Some people prepare a balance sheet once a year. I do it every month because I want to know where my financial position is at any given moment. By doing this, I am able to control my expenses better when they get out of control, which they sometimes do. Then, during the next month, I can cut back and get back on track. I don't have to wait one year when it may too late.

It also helps me pinpoint where I can save and add to my retirement. Remember, if you are in the 50% tax bracket, for every dollar you spend, it takes $2 pretax to spend $1 after tax. In Figure 3, I provide a simple income statement.

Figure 3

Expense Worksheet

Estimated Monthly Expenses

Item	Now	Retirement
Rent or Lease Payment	$5,000	$0
Food and Household	1,225	1,225
Utilities	400	400
Auto Related	1,000	600
Clothing, Personal Items	300	200
Domestic Help	200	0
Property Taxes	479	479
Entertainment	350	500
Charitable Contributions	200	100
Books and Subscription	100	150
Home Furnishings	100	50
Gifts	200	400
Medical Expenses	700	1300
Other Expenses	200	200
Life Insurance Premiums	300	200
Medical Insurance Premiums	400	600
House Insurance	200	200
Other Insurance	100	150
Total	**$11,454**	**$6,754**

The income statement in Figure 3 shows us that expenses in retirement have declined from $11,454 per month to $6,754 (a drop of 40%), primarily due to paying off the house loan. If the house loan was not paid off (which many retirees do not do), the expenses after retirement are roughly the same as before retirement. In other words, outside the home loan, retirement expenses are usually the same. The estimated expenses in retirement do not factor in inflation. A good financial calculator (such as the one I have on my Web site at **www.stevensfirstprinciples.com**) will help you project your estimated expenses.

At least once a year, update this information and chart your progress or lack thereof. To stay on a good retirement track, your investment assets need to grow at the rate you have determined by using Figure 1 or the 6% conservative rate many planners use.

For example, I've chosen 6% as my rate of return, so my investments need to grow more or less at that rate. However, your investment assets will not grow at an even pace. In some years, your return might only be 4.5%; in others, it might be 7% or 8%, which is one of the reasons you can't fret about month-to-month or year-to-year ebbs in your portfolio. However, if you're off track for any considerable length of time (e.g., 3 years or more), you should make adjustments that will put you back on course.

Not saving enough money has proven to be a trap for many who dreamed of a comfortable retirement. Pension plans and Social Security will not provide enough on which to live. As an example, defined benefit pension plans are not indexed for inflation, and defined contribution plans usually provide a lump sum payout upon retirement.

We have already discussed how the government is grossly miscalculating Social Security's liabilities (they have already raised the minimum age and reduced the amount of benefits in a losing effort to keep pace). In addition, this once sacred agreement between the government and its citizens is being pilfered for a plethora of other government spending (they were never supposed to be able to borrow from the Social Security fund, but they do…and they do so freely).

Less Gold in the Golden Years

It sometimes seems the world, or at least our financial world, is falling apart around us. We can't count on Social Security, and now we can't even count on our pension plans because this once sacrosanct cushion is going the way of the Enron's of the world.

A recent *Orange County Register* column—entitled "Employees and retirees fret that United's proposal to end pension plans will start a trend" — stated…

> *The issue is money, specifically pension income.*
>
> *United retirees and workers are facing the prospect of losing a good portion of their retirement money if the airline follows through with a proposal to terminate its pension program to shore up its teetering finances.*
>
> *If that happens, the Pension Benefit Guaranty Corp., a quasi-government agency created to oversee troubled pension plans, would take over the United Pension, but half or more would cut payments — potentially.*
>
> *It's an issue being played out again and again across the country as companies, burdened by high pension costs, increasingly are opting to end their plans, leaving their workers scrambling to find a way to fill what could be a very big hole in their retirement finances….*

In other words, you're on your own. The truth is that you need to spend less and save more.

 **Follow the Herd**

Investors love to follow the herd. The dot-com bust was a perfect example. If so many people are doing it, and getting rich (investors tell themselves), then I should be investing in tech, too — which, as previously stated, is currently the same thinking going on in real estate.

"A fool would rather be deceived than disturbed."

–Anonymous

However, going along with the crowd may not always be the right thing to do. In fact, more often than not, investors with good instincts who "go against the grain," are the ones who reap the biggest rewards.

Moreover, it's not just individuals who run with the herd. It's the large institutional investors like mutual and retirement funds. Between March 2000 and March 2003, many portfolios had declined from 40% to 60% or more. Ouch! Some Internet "laden" funds and portfolios suffered far greater pains, on the magnitude of 90%.

Significant declines and losses are not reserved for the stock market alone. According to the UCLA *Anderson Economic Forecast,* portions of the Los Angeles and Orange County real estate markets declined by more than 20% between 1990 and 1995. In San Fernando Valley, California, it was far worse, with some areas losing up to 40%. During the same timeframe, real estate declined by more than 20% in Newport Beach, California.

Odds are that the investors who now shun stocks and jump into real estate, without any experience, will suffer the same bad results they did with the stock market.

At the peak of the 1990 real estate bubble one of my clients started buying residential property in Southern Orange County hoping to make a quick profit by flipping houses. Unfortunately, his timing was off, and he was nearly wiped out. Today, in 2004, I am seeing the same scenario repeating itself.

In the early 1980s, speculators believed that gold would go to $2,000 an ounce, but quickly found out they were wrong. Some purchased gold and silver with every dime they had, only to lose everything shortly thereafter.

The famous Hunt brothers of Texas lost their entire formidable fortune betting incorrectly that silver would exceed $50 an ounce.

It is difficult not to follow the herd. It is part of our social nature to want to be a part of a group. We learn this early on in school and continue to follow those learned behaviors well into adult life. It is especially difficult not to follow, when those who seem to be leading are doing so well. We humans would rather be wrong together than be right by ourselves.

Inflation—The Hidden Tax

When I graduated from college in 1977, I was making $12,000 a year, which I thought was a lot of money. Today, I earn many times that amount, yet I have no greater buying power, dollar for dollar, than I did then. The culprit? Inflation. In 1971, my father bought me a "Super Beetle" Volkswagen, which cost him $1,300. Today, the same car costs $21,000.

"Inflation might be called legalized counterfeiting."

–Irvin Fisher, 'Stabilizing the Dollar,' 1920

The difference in cost for a Volkswagen Beetle between 1971 and 2004 works out to be about 4.5% per year. When you look at inflation on a short-term basis, such as year-to-year, it doesn't seem so bad. However, on a longer term, even a moderate inflation, such as 4.5%, can add up and devastate one's retirement plans.

If you're planning on your upcoming salary increase to reduce the ravages of inflation — rethink your plan. Over the past 50 years, inflation has averaged 4% a year, and most salary increases have been about the same. The result? You're running in place or on a treadmill. In other words, your purchasing power has remained stagnant.

In fact, when you factor in State and Federal income taxes, property taxes, increased sales taxes, etc., you're most likely not even staying even.

Inaccurate Government Statistics

The net result of all this is that inflation is eroding the wealth of our fellow Americans, or at least most of them, and the government's statistics don't begin to tell the truth about it. For example, the Consumer Price Index for the year 2003 showed that inflation climbed just 1.8%. However, the method they use to calculate the "housing" component is flawed and does not correctly register the increase in housing prices.

While the government reported no inflation, anyone with even a bit of common sense who was trying to purchase a home in 2003, could readily see the effects of inflation.

The government also likes to exclude food and energy in its inflation calculations, claiming these figures are "too volatile" to accurately gauge true inflation. I don't know about you, but I like to eat, and I need to drive, and maybe I'll be buying a new home next year. For me, not including the effects of inflation on these items would be sheer folly. Bill Gross, the celebrated PIMCO Bond Manager, wrote in his October, 2004, newsletter to clients that the inflation rate, as calculated by the U.S. Government, was understated by at least 1%. As do I, Gross believes that the government understates the inflation rate.

Why doesn't the government include these items? Because it's not to their advantage to keep inflation statistics subdued. Why? Because the cost of living adjustments to everything from Social Security to Medicare would reflect an expensive reality.

People who intentionally give bad advice generally have a hidden, self-serving agenda.

If you're like the majority of investors, you want safety combined with capital appreciation, but the truth is, there are no guarantees. You need to save more and be smarter with your investments, which is the only guarantee you're going to get. Take for example, a U.S. Treasury bill. Would you consider this a risk-free investment? Most people would. The truth is that T-bills are NOT risk free, at least not from the standpoint of inflation. According to the *Wall Street Journal*, the U.S. Treasury Note due February 2005 is yielding 1.7% and, as of this writing, inflation is running 2.8%.

Inflation Is Not Going Away

Unfortunately, inflation is a permanent reality because of the currency system the world now uses. In the past, before 1913, when the world was on the gold standard, inflation was not as problematic. According to Sidney Homer's *History of Inflation*, "Inflation averaged under 1% for the 200 years preceding 1925."

However, ever since the creation of the U.S. Federal Reserve in 1913, inflation has adjusted itself upwards. Inflation was at its worst in 1921, when the rate was 15% a year. While at a 5% average since 1925, it ultimately peaked at 13% in 1981.

Unless the world returns to a gold standard, we can expect inflation to be part of our daily lives. Therefore, we need to factor it into our saving, spending, and investment way of thinking because inflation — even in small doses — erodes the value of our money.

Identity Theft
It Takes a Thief

The **government steals** the value of your money through inflation and robs you of your retirement through reduced Social Security benefits, and then criminals want what's left. The sophistication of criminals and the increased use of technology (i.e., the Internet) have made identity theft easier than ever. According to a KNX 1070 News Radio broadcast, there were 7,000,000 cases of computer fraud in 2003, and that number is expected to go beyond 9,000,000 this year (2004).

> **"Never trust anyone who says, 'Trust me.'"**
>
> –Anonymous

It is also estimated that one in every five credit card holders will have an unauthorized use of his or her card every three years.

A friend of mine recently had his mail stolen from his mailbox. It contained eight bills he was paying. He wasn't aware that the mail had been stolen until creditors began to call him asking for payments. By then, four weeks had passed, and his identity had already been stolen and used continuously. It was easy for the criminals because his mail contained account numbers, bank numbers, his address, and his name. Of course, my friend closed his accounts and started new ones, but the thieves didn't need to access his accounts. They only needed his name and address. With this information they were able to go online and in less than a minute, for only $20, they had his Social Security number and were free to begin opening new bank and credit card accounts in his name. Most honest people don't understand that with the Internet and very little expertise, anyone can find your Social Security number with just your name and address.

Needless to say, my friend's experience is still an ongoing nightmare. It is extremely difficult to prove you are not the one opening bank accounts or applying for credit cards. We all need to take prudent steps to prevent identity theft. It is crucial to protecting your assets and, ultimately, your retirement. My friend had to contact all three credit bureaus and ask them to put a "fraud alert" — which automatically stays in force for the next five years — on his accounts. When this happens, anyone who applies for credit using his name will have to supply several forms of identity (not difficult for a criminal), and they will have to supply very personal information in order to prove that they are who they say they are, such as mother's maiden name, name of a pet, birth date, etc. Unfortunately, my friend now has to do the same every time he applies for credit.

According to *Smart Money* magazine, U.S. authorities have caught hundreds of illegal immigrants who have stolen Social Security cards to get jobs. That gave these unscrupulous people access to high security areas at airports around the country under false pretenses. Still others have gained access to brokerage accounts and banks using Social Security numbers and other identification obtained from customer records when they were stolen from unsecured depositories.

Criminals rummage through garbage cans and bins, often finding incredibly sensitive materials such as canceled checks, bills, and letters from which they glean valuable information to steal your identity. For this reason, it would not be a bad idea to purchase a paper shredder. We all inadvertently throw away personal information on an almost daily basis, never thinking that someone might be rifling through our trash late at night.

Some Useful Tips to Prevent Being Ripped Off

The key to keep from being ripped off is *being aware*. Now that you know how easy it is to locate your Social Security number (the keys to the kingdom of fraud), you can take steps to protect yourself. Never give your Social Security number to someone you don't know, or if you sense that a business is not legitimate. If a clerk asks for your Social Security number for identification to purchase something with a check, you should refuse to provide it. There is no reason for a retail store to have your Social Security number. For example, I was buying some books over the Internet in Costa Rica and the company asked me for my Social Security and passport numbers, claiming they needed them for documentation purposes before they shipped the goods. Being wary, I gave them phony numbers. (I was not about to give them my true Social Security and passport numbers!)

Do *not* give your Social Security number to anyone over the Internet that does not represent a reputable business using encrypted technology. If in doubt, pass up the urge to purchase.

In 2003, there was a rash of frauds by thieves who set up bogus Web sites resembling the one Citibank offers, enticing people to give them personal information. They were successful in draining many unsuspecting individuals' bank accounts.

Never carry your Social Security card with you. Keep it in a safe place, preferably under lock and key. As an alternate, it's far better to memorize the number.

At the risk of sounding paranoid, you should *never* give your Social Security number to anyone using a cellular phone. Cellular phones are unsecured, and it is relatively easy for criminals to eavesdrop on conversations.

Do you have a Palm Pilot or similar PDA device? Do you keep credit card information, passwords, account information, or your Social Security number on it? Avoid doing this if you can. If not, at least put a protective password on your PDA.

You should also review your monthly bills and bank statements very carefully for charges with which you are not familiar. If you find suspicious activity, contact the bank or applicable company and report it immediately. If there has been an unauthorized check or charge and you report it within 60 days, most financial institutions have to correct the error and make you financially whole again.

On one occasion, Anderson Cooper, the CNN anchor, didn't check his bank statement for over 90 days. Unfortunately, someone had written checks on his account and he lost $30,000. The bank told him: "Sorry. You didn't report this within 60 days. We are no longer responsible."

The same applies to your brokerage statements. Keep a wary lookout for any changes in balances, that dividends are properly credited, and the securities in your account are actually there — and in the same amounts as the previous month.

Credit card companies, mortgage brokers, banks, and others constantly flood our mailboxes with solicitations for financial products, which is another breeding ground for fraud. A criminal can either steal these from your unlocked mailbox or retrieve them from your trash.

It is also a good idea to check each of the three credit reporting companies — Experian, TransUnion, and Equifax — every quarter (I check them monthly through an automated service they offer). The easiest way to check your credit is to go to any one of them, and for a nominal fee, you can get a complete report [from all three], online, within minutes.

A Brief Look at Insurance and Estate Planning

The various forms of insurance available today are important tools in protecting you from unwanted risk and in helping you reach your financial goals. Obviously, life insurance protects a family in the event of the death of that family's provider. There are also policies to protect you in the event you can't work and, of course, having at least a major medical health insurance policy can protect you from catastrophic financial losses in the event of major illnesses or accidents.

> "If it were not for lawyers, we wouldn't need them."
>
> –A.K. Griffen, 'Lawyers Paradox'

This section is designed as strictly an overview to provide you, the investor, with a very basic primer on what types of insurance are most necessary. Space does not permit an in-depth review of estate planning or an all-inclusive list of the insurance options available to you. Because insurance can be tricky, you should consult with a qualified insurance professional.

Property, Casualty, and Liability Insurance

Everyone should have some basic liability coverage, which, while inexpensive, is critical protection against lawsuits covering a wide array of potential problems: Someone slips on your doorstep and breaks a leg; your dog bites a neighbor; a strong wind blows a tree down in your backyard into your neighbor's.

I was driving through Beverly Hills one day, turning left, when an unlicensed driver plowed into me. I called the police immediately, who cited the other driver for not having a license or insurance. As simple as this scenario seemed, it wasn't. Even though I had the right of way, the other driver called an attorney later and sued my insurance company (even though he wasn't licensed or insured!), claiming that *he* had the right of way. Ironically, my insurance company paid the driver off, finding it cheaper to do that than to go through the time and costs involved with a court case.

I recommend to my clients that they carry liability insurance in excess of the basic minimums on their cars, homes, and rental properties. You never know what attorney may decide to go after your "deep pockets." Any good insurance agent can provide you with what is called an "excess" or "umbrella" policy, which should give you coverage of at least 1 ½ times your net worth. For example, if your net worth is $5,000,000 then get coverage for $7,500,000. Umbrella policies are not expensive. For example, a $10,000,000 policy costs about $1,000 a year. Also consider maximum uninsured/underinsured motorist insurance.

In addition, of course, you should carry fire insurance and, especially in California, earthquake insurance, the minimum limits of which should — at the very least — cover the replacement of your home and its contents.

Life Insurance

The most obvious purpose of life insurance is to protect against the loss of income if the income earner passes away. It can also be used to reduce estate taxes.

Because this specialized field requires a solid base of knowledge and sophistication, it is advisable that you investigate and choose a competent agent.

Many people are led to believe that insurance is an investment, or they are told they need much more coverage than they actually do. My personal opinion is that insurance is used to protect someone against very specific and general risks. I have a friend who sells life insurance for a living and recommends that his clients buy a lot of it for protection, but he himself, has little life insurance. This alone tells me a lot about life insurance. If you need life insurance, I suggest you purchase a "term" policy for the period that your risk is exposed. For example, if you're married and have a newborn, you might want to get a 20-year level term policy to protect your family in case something happens to you.

Term life insurance does not build cash value, but it is far cheaper than "whole life" or "universal life" policies that do. You would be better off investing the difference in something that offers greater returns, which is not difficult to do. Whole life and universal life policies are expensive because they offer a death benefit, as well as an investment benefit. Unfortunately, the returns are low. For one thing, management fees take away from the returns, and the value builds too slowly. Generally, the rate of return on these types of policies is only 2% to 3%. You can do far better on your own. However, certain circumstances require whole life insurance, or a variation of it; therefore, it is wise to consult an estate planning attorney who is familiar with insurance trusts before buying anything but term insurance.

Using life insurance for estate planning is another story. For the most part, it is worthwhile, but this is a specialized field that requires an estate-planning attorney who is very knowledgeable and has the in-depth expertise with current laws and tax codes. Frankly, many attorneys don't bother to stay current on these matters. So, choose your lawyer carefully and ask for references from satisfied clients.

Health and Long-Term Care Insurance

Two very important words about health insurance — *get it!* Personally, I prefer a PPO so that I can choose my own doctor. We are all aware of how high the costs for health care policies are. However, a few words to the wise should suffice: With just a few days' stay in a hospital, a single accident or serious health problem can literally wipe you out financially!

If you aren't insured, the doctors and hospital, just like any other large creditor, will come after all your assets to satisfy payment.

"Long-term care" — which is probably one of the most often overlooked forms of protection for your assets — is another type of health insurance that you should at least consider.

We don't think about it often, but if you or a loved one becomes incapacitated or seriously ill — to the extent that you must be placed in a nursing home — these costs, just like with any other catastrophic illness, can decimate your finances. Costs to care for an individual in a long-term care facility can run as high as $10,000 a month!

This type coverage can be purchased while you're in your 50s, for an intended stay of 3 to 5 years. Statistics show that most people who go into a nursing home usually stay for three years or less — and they recover or they die. With at least a 5% inflation factored in, purchase the maximum coverage you can afford.

When you purchase long-term health insurance, buy from a company with a strong record for paying their claims. Every policy has a set of guidelines that trigger admittance into a long-term care facility. Be sure to read the fine print carefully and know what rules and restrictions apply. Some policies are too rigid in their restrictions, making it difficult to comply.

At this time, I would recommend GE Capital or Northwestern. Of course, just like any other insurance, you have to do your homework to determine if the company has the financial ability to pay its claims. You can find insurance company ratings in *A.M. Best Rates*, a reference book available at most libraries. Stick with carriers rated "A" or better. Do your homework, and talk with someone you can trust. Don't rely on an insurance agent who wants to sell you a policy, regardless of what it will cost, or whether or not it is right for you.

Other forms of insurance such as extended auto warranties or home appliance warranties are, in my opinion, a waste of money. For example, most people don't keep a car long enough to warrant the purchase of a 100,000 mile or 5-year extended warranty. Moreover, most home appliances are so well built, these warranties are a waste of money. However, they are very profitable for those who sell them. Use the extra cash to invest in something that will earn you some money.

Estate Planning

Excellent estate planning attorneys aren't cheap, but in the end, they are well worth the cost.

There are countless people who neglect to get their wills updated, even though they may have formed a trust. Trusts are critical in minimizing taxes and passing assets along to spouses and heirs. A living trust will allow your estate to be passed to your heirs without the hassle, cost, and time of probate.

Again, it is necessary to seek well-qualified trust and estate planning attorneys in this complex area. In addition, beware of "trusts in a kit" or attorneys who claim they can draw up a trust for as little as $800. A good and decent trust, drawn up by a competent attorney, costs a minimum of $2,500. Some trusts that are more complex can cost much more.

A final note: Don't forget to call your IRA custodian and change the beneficiary of your IRA to the person you want designated. Many IRA owners forget to do this, most often when they marry. It is a good idea to periodically check with the custodian and/or financial advisor to make sure the beneficiary of your IRA is current and consistent with your circumstances at any given time.

I have only scratched the surface here on the subject of insurance. If you need coverage, seek out a reputable agent. Ask your friends for referrals. Make sure your agent has been in the business for a long time. Remember, it's best to buy insurance from specialists and knowledgeable people, not brokers who are generalists interested only in commissions.

The Investor and His Advisor
Looking for Mr. Goodwrench

There are nearly as many types of investment advisors as there are investments, and it can be difficult to choose the right one and decide on what is a fair cost for their services.

Although this book is designed to guide you in implementing your own investment plan, I realize that some investors don't have the time — or the inclination — to do this on their own.

A good advisor is in demand and is often busy. For this reason, the exceptional advisors will not consult with a potential client, or manage their money, if the investor doesn't meet the advisor's minimums for assets under management.

Size Does Matter

Except for special circumstances, my firm, Stevens First Principles Investment Advisors, does not accept accounts under $250,000, which is our stated minimum. However, in all honesty, we aren't interested in accounts with less than $500,000 in assets. This is not arrogance on our part; it is merely a fact of business life. Our most precious commodities are *knowledge* and *time*, and we can only serve so many clients well.

A bad advisor is one who is a mass marketer and has an army of salesmen touting his advisory services. For example, I hear an advisor on the radio touting his investment and financial planning services, offering free financial plans and consultations to the first 10 callers to his radio show.

A competent financial advisor knows that to do a credible service for a client takes time, and that the advisor cannot perform a thorough financial analysis for someone in 10 minutes.

Another advisor advertises his services on the Internet and then sends his troops to make the sales call. Unfortunately, a lot of unsuspecting people fall for these types of sales, the results of which are not pretty!

Managed Accounts

If you use an independent advisor, look for one that advises clients with over $200 million in managed assets, but has less than $1 billion under management. When advisors become too large, their performance starts to suffer because, out of necessity, they have to move into larger capitalization stocks for liquidity.

You should expect the advisor to assign you a relationship manager, who should not have more than 100 clients to service. If you are going to pay the advisor's fee, you should expect service and performance in return.

Organizations with assets larger than $2 billion experience what is called "portfolio drift" as they move from small and mid-capitalization stocks to larger, more liquid stocks. Therefore, a good advisor will limit his number of clients and the amount of money he has under management to ensure that his performance is satisfactory.

Active managers are advisors who attempt to beat the market, while passive managers use an approach to try to match the market. More will be said later about the pros and cons of both approaches to investing.

There are good advisors available to you, but it will take some investigation on your part to find them. Through their investment representatives, many brokerage firms have consultant's on-staff who maintain databases of qualified managers with whom they can place their client's money.

Although using a broker in what is called a managed account program is better than you choosing a bad money manager this service is not free — nor is it cheap. Some brokers charge anywhere from .70 of 1%, to 1%, to choose a money manager for you. Others will charge as much as 1.25% or more. Since most brokers don't monitor the manger's performance as closely as they should, especially on accounts under $1,000,000, this service can be expensive.

For any advisor that uses active management, you should not pay more than 1.25% if your assets under management are less than $1,000,000. For amounts above $1,000,000, you should not pay more than 1%. You can find plenty of competent advisors that will do a good job for a reasonable fee.

For passive management, the key to good investment performance is to keep fees and expenses low. There are a number of passive managers out there who charge an outrageous investment advisory fee for very little work. I ran across an advisor recently who uses a passive investment approach and charges 1% annually for basically doing very little. With this particular advisor, once the account is set up, he rebalances the portfolio once a year — that's it. He really should not charge more than .50 of 1%. For the 1% fee, he should be actively managing his portfolios, but I suspect that would entail too much work for him.

Using the portfolio models in this book will generally work as well as using a broker to locate a money manager for your portfolio or using a bad advisor.

For the wealthy, brokerage firms such as UBS, Merrill Lynch, and Morgan Stanley have wealth advisory units that help the investor with advice and financial planning. However, remember that most of the so-called financial consultants at these firms are paid to sell, not necessarily manage your money well.

Depending upon the asset size under management, there are also different levels of service. Banks and trust banks such as Citicorp, U.S Trust, and Northern Trust offer this service.

However, by using either a broker or a bank, you will increase the amount of fees you pay, hence lowering returns on your assets.

Regardless, if you use a brokerage or a bank, you should make the asset allocation decisions yourself with the guidance of this book, or at least retain a large part of the decision-making responsibilities.

Always check your advisor's ADV filings with the U.S. Securities and Exchange Commission (SEC). Obviously, it's a given that you wouldn't want an advisor who has serious blemishes on his record. The SEC regulates advisors with $25,000,000 or more in assets, while state regulatory agencies watch those with less than this amount under management. In my opinion, it is better to choose an advisor who manages more than $25,000,000 because he or she generally has more experience and is scrutinized by the SEC (and the SEC's requirements are more stringent than that of state authorities).

Every advisor, regardless of size, should have "malfeasance insurance," which protects the client in case the advisor decides to disappear with his clients' funds. Ask the advisor for a copy of this insurance rider and then call the insurance company to be certain it is in force.

Caution: Malfeasance insurance does *not* protect the client if the advisor makes bad investment decisions. There are a number of very bad advisors out there, some of whom make poor decisions. Use only advisors who have errors and omissions insurance in the minimum amount of at least $1,000,000. If your assets exceed that amount, you should use an advisor who has a policy that provides coverage for at least the amount you have under management with the advisor.

Ask for proof of insurance and, again, call the insurance company to make sure the policy is in force. As a reminder, the insurance company underwriting the policy should have an "A" rating by *A.M. Best*. Your state insurance commissioner can also tell you what rating the insurance company has.

Beware that some small advisors are part of a broker-dealer affiliation, which can lead to conflicts of interest because the advisor may be tempted to trade through his affiliated broker, which may not mean you'll be getting the best prices. These prices may be higher than what you would pay to an independent advisor or a large brokerage firm, which I think is the best arrangement.

Insist that your assets be held in custody at a large, well-known and respected trust company or a large independent custodian, such as Charles Schwab or Fidelity. If you need the services of a trust company, I recommend U.S. Trust, an old-line blue chip trust bank, or Fiduciary International Trust, which is part of the Franklin-Templeton group.

Do not agree to pool your assets with those of the advisory firm or any other clients, unless you are in a hedge fund type of investment. Insist that each custodian have insurance from a well-regarded and financially sound private insurance company to the extent of your investments with that custodian.

Securities Investor Protection Corp. (SIPC) is a quasi-government agency, which insures brokerage accounts up to $500,000. If you have more money than that under management, your custodian should provide private insurance. If he or she doesn't do so, move your account to someone who does.

All of your securities should be placed in cash accounts — not in margin accounts. A margin account is one that allows you to borrow money or permits the brokerage firm to loan out your securities. Most people don't even realize that their securities are being lent to others by their broker. When you sign up for margin you give the broker permission to lend out your securities. By keeping your stocks and bonds in a cash account you have an extra layer of protection in case your brokerage firm collapses because your securities won't be lent out. U.S. Treasury Securities can be held in custody directly with the Federal Reserve, as can Savings Bonds; however, most people prefer to keep Savings Bonds in a safe deposit box.

What should you look for in an advisor?

I suggest that the advisor have a minimum of 10 continuous years of experience, either analyzing securities or working with securities directly. Today, many firms, both large and small, are in the business of gathering assets so that they can charge fees. It is rare that you would ever be able to talk directly with the person investing your money.

You would normally be assigned a "relationship manager" as a contact. If you're a seasoned investor, you might get a seasoned relationship manager, while those with smaller assets generally end up with someone "fresh in the business."

Insist on a seasoned professional.

According to the International Association of Registered Financial Consultants, there are 87 designations for people working in the financial services industries sponsored by 85 organizations. These designations can be confusing, and each one has specific educational requirements. You can find a list of these designations and their definitions at **www.iarfc.com**, **www.fp.edu**, or **www.nasd.org**.

Just because an individual has a professional designation doesn't mean that he or she is qualified. For example, the Certified Financial Planner® designation is awarded to those participants who pass a rigorous examination and have experience in the financial services industries. However, there are many CFP® planners who are nothing more than salesmen of insurance and mutual funds and don't have an in-depth knowledge of investments. Don't get me wrong — many CFP® practitioners are very good, but make sure you find one who has an in-depth knowledge of mutual funds and investments.

In all fairness, as with anything else, there are many good planners but there are bad ones as well. The point is, don't choose an advisor based on a designation.

Another popular designation is the CFA, as awarded by the CFA Institute. The CFA charter holder passes a rigorous examination and has to have at least a Bachelors Degree from an accredited university. Although the CFA holder is knowledgeable about modern portfolio theory and financial analysis, some of them are mediocre advisors. Working with students at UCLA, I've had the opportunity to observe hundreds of students who have trained to be security analysts. In the CFA, they are taught to be excellent analysts, not stock pickers who can think outside the herd. I don't want to detract from the CFA credential, because it is very difficult to earn, but what I am saying is that credentials by themselves don't mean much. A long track record of being in business and performance matters more.

Professionals who have earned either the Chartered Mutual Fund Counselor Designation or Certified Fund Specialist usually have a good knowledge of mutual funds, asset allocation, portfolio management, and risk control. These designations require experience and passing a rigorous examination before certificate holders are awarded the designations. But, here again, there are good ones as well as bad ones.

In the early 1950s, Walter Schloss of Walter and Edwin Schloss and Associates studied at the New York Institute of Finance under Benjamin Graham. Having only taken a few courses, he had no college degree at all; yet, his record is astounding.

Warren Buffett and George Soros have college degrees, but no professional designations, and they are undisputedly the top two greatest investors of all time.

Remember, credentials are important, but not in and of themselves. A proven history and record of accomplishment of successful investing with honesty over a period of 10 or more years is far more important than credentials or titles.

What Not to Look For In an Advisor

I have a client who selected his former broker because he drove a Porsche and had a trophy wife. Unfortunately, the broker's taste in cars and women did not keep him from losing more than 60% of my client's portfolio value before he came to me for advice.

Do not choose an advisor because he appears to be doing well.

The Fallacy of Market Timing

In order to retire comfortably, you need to attain a certain amount of assets, which requires good, long-term performance. Some advisors believe they can beat the market by timing the purchase and sale of securities, or by darting in and out of the markets.

This is rarely a prescription for obtaining wealth. If you look at some of the accomplished investors like Warren Buffett or George Soros who have accumulated substantial wealth, much of it came from being a long-term investor and not trying to buy and sell at every market turn.

Don't be misled by advisors telling you that long-term investing is dead and the only way to make profits is by trading. Benjamin Graham, who Warren Buffett once called the greatest investor of the twentieth century, proved beyond a doubt that long-term investing works — and that it works well.

Regardless of whether you use an advisor, or you act on your own behalf, you should follow the principles in this book if you want to retire comfortably with a simple, inexpensive plan.

Banks and Brokerages

Banks, trust banks, insurance companies, brokerage firms, and mutual fund companies all provide a variety of investment services.

Generally — and for good reason — banks don't offer much in terms of quality relationships or low costs. Experienced and seasoned financial professionals don't work at banks because they can command a far greater income elsewhere or on their own.

The result is that commercial banks use young advisors without much experience and/or experienced advisors that perform poorly. Banks are also notorious for pushing products to their customers. The products they want to sell you generate high fees for the bank, but don't always produce the results you may want.

Trust companies, though not perfect, are better than commercial banks. Although they pay their portfolio managers less than brokerage firms and traditional money managers, they are accustomed to dealing with wealthy clients, and they act accordingly.

Usually, the minimum asset portfolio at a trust company is $1 million. A recent trend at these firms and brokerages is a "managed account platform," where instead of an institution such as a trust bank or brokerage managing money, the trust sub-contracts the money management out to investment advisors; and, of course, they add fees for you to have the "privilege" of having your money managed by an outsider.

If you are willing to pay this fee, request that they use my diversification guidelines (which you'll find later in this book). Believe me, you'll worry less about your account and sleep better at night. Trust managers will monitor these sub-contractors and report their performance to you. And ask them to reduce their fee if they use one of my models. It means that they will invest using the passive approach.

Warning! One of my clients has a "Charitable Remainder" trust at a leading trust bank, and I am responsible for the supervision of this account.

I've had numerous meetings with the portfolio manager responsible for the investments and have constantly lectured him regarding his poor performance. I would have fired him long ago were it not for the fact that my client's attorney is one of their larger referral sources, and he won't allow my client to give me permission to terminate their services — a conflict of interest to be sure, and a situation about which I've apprised my client.

My grandfather left me $10,000 in 1969 and had a well-known bank manage it in trust until I turned 21. When I reached this age in 1975, the bank had turned the $10,000 into $3,000. At the time, I didn't understand what a trust was supposed to accomplish. Even though a trust bank seems strong, conservative, and safe, you must carefully monitor their asset allocation and performance; and when they don't perform, they must be terminated. Another tip would be to spread your assets out among two or three trust banks. If you use a trust company or brokerage that uses a managed account program, you will have to monitor them for performance and cost.

You should also be aware of fly-by-night trust companies, especially those located outside the United States or others domiciled in Nevada — many of which are not safe.

Are There Any Good Brokers Left?

It used to be that a stockbroker was trusted like the family physician or a trusted accountant, but those days are over. My father had such a broker, who did well for him for many years. However, today, although it can be done, it is difficult to find a broker who is more interested in his client's welfare than in lining his own pockets with commissions and fees.

Ed Satlin of Deutsche Bank has been a broker for over 40 years, and he treats each client's money as if it were his own. Although Deutsche Bank utilizes managed account platforms, a broker like Ed will invest as his clients direct him.

Ed is an exception. A broker is more often than not going to want to generate commissions; after all, that's how he makes his living.

The newest product that is being sold by brokers these days is the "fund of funds" concept which, in mutual funds, has been around for a long time. Essentially, a fund of funds is a packaged group of mutual funds that has exposure to several asset classes and sub-sectors. The idea is to assemble a group of mutual funds that have portfolio managers that the sponsoring organization believes can outperform the market.

Fund of funds have had a terrible history of performance throughout the years and are layered with management fees. You would be better off indexing your portfolio, using several index fund sub-sectors. The latest reincarnation of this concept is being used to assemble a fund of hedge funds, which I predict will end as badly as the fund of funds concept.

Mutual Funds

Choosing a good "discount" broker is a much simpler choice. Quality firms include Charles Schwab and Fidelity Investments. Commissions are low, service is excellent, and trades are well executed. Most importantly, they are honest.

The record clearly shows that most load mutual funds cannot beat their proposed benchmark, so why use a load fund at all? With the exception of specialty funds such as Pimco's All Asset

Fund (PASDX) or Pimco's Real Return Commodity Index Fund (PCRDX), there is no need to use load funds. They are sold by brokers and financial planners to generate commissions.

Loads (costs) range from 4% to 7%. By paying these loads, essentially, right from the get-go, you've lost 4% to 7% of your principal. No load funds have no sales charges, and all of your money goes directly to work in the fund. With so many Exchange traded funds and no-load funds available, there is no reason to pay fees.

If you choose to use a no-load fund instead of Exchange traded funds, then you should pick strong mutual funds with good long-term performance records and a history of low fees and turnover rates.

Higher fees and turnover transaction costs will act as an anchor and put some "portfolio drag" on your returns, so you need to compare management fees and other costs with similar funds in the same sub-sector. Obviously, you should choose funds with low fees, turnover rates, and excellent performance records over a fund with higher fees. *Morningstar's Guide on Mutual Funds* should be very helpful when making these comparisons. You can sign on with them online at **www.morningstar.com** and receive daily updates.

Also, keep in mind that performance numbers can be misleading, depending upon which period the advisor uses. For example, one recent advertisement that I read boasted about a particular fund's one-year performance, but the timeframe they chose was a period in which their results looked great if compared with a standardized period.

With a little effort, a simple investment plan can be implemented by anyone. However, I realize many investors feel more comfortable when they have guidance. If you want some guidance, then I suggest that you use a large, well-respected trust bank or several independent advisors with excellent reputations and good, long-term track records. Their costs might eat into your profits somewhat, but it may be worth your peace of mind.

Though history doesn't exactly repeat itself, it's safe to use it wisely to help you obtain favorable results in the future. By using historical data and investing for the long-term (i.e., 5 to 10 years), you can achieve financial security and save for retirement.

The Performance of Different Assets

There are periods when certain asset classes do well and other times when these same classes do poorly. Looking at the data below from Ibbotson Associates, stocks in any 10-year period since 1920 had negative returns in only one period: the 1930s. Since this decade (2000) is not over, it is too early to determine if this performance period will be negative.

The 1930s — which, of course, included the Great Depression — reduced the value of all asset classes, as did the first four years of the 2000s, except for bonds, real estate, and commodities.

However, during all other periods, stocks have had a positive return (see Figure 4 below). Even during the '70s, when economic malaise and stagflation were present, large company equities returned 5.9% annualized, while small company stocks delivered 11.5%

> **"Investment must be rational. If you can't understand it, don't do it."**
>
> –Warren Buffett, as quoted by Janet Lowe

Figure 4
Compound Annual Rates of Return by Decade

	1920s	1930s	1940s	1950s	1960s	1970s	1980s	1990s	2000
Large Cap									
	19.2	-0.1	9.2	19.4	7.8	5.9	17.5	18.2	-5.3

	1920s	1930s	1940s	1950s	1960s	1970s	1980s	1990s	2000
Small Cap									
	-4.5	1.4	20.7	16.9	15.5	11.5	15.8	15.1	13.3
Corporate									
	5.2	6.9	2.7	1.0	1.7	6.2	13	8.4	11.2
Treasury Bills									
	3.7	0.6	0.4	1.9	3.9	6.3	8.9	4.9	3.1
Inflation									
	-1.1	-2.0	5.4	2.2	2.5	7.4	5.1	2.9	2.3

Source: Ibbotson and Associates SBBI Yearbook

Everyone's goal should be to retire comfortably, so investors need to outpace inflation. You can see from the above data that during two decades in the past eight, T-Bills have not kept up with inflation.

During periods of deflation, T-Bills provide a very nice real rate of return, as they did in the 1920s and 1930s. Although U.S. Treasury Securities are safer than corporate bonds or stocks, for most periods, they do not outpace inflation.

When T-Bills did outpace inflation it was because the Federal Reserve reduced interest rates dramatically during this time and inflation was, likewise, reduced.

However, in 2004, the situation is different with inflation running — at the time of this writing (October 2004) — at a 2.8% annual clip, while T-Bills are paying 1.79%. Investors that bought short-term T-Bills are now getting a negative rate of return.

The rates of inflation have always been volatile. If you examine the data in Figure 4 above, you can see that inflation rates change over time — from year-to-year and decade-to-decade.

During times of deflation and contraction of the money supply and credit, inflation is greatly reduced. In Figure 4 above you can see that inflation was actually negative only in one decade in the past eight.

When the Federal Reserve expands the money supply and the growth of credit, inflation ensues. It was especially insidious during the 1940s and '50s, then again during the '70s and '80s, and finally during 1980 through 1990.

From 1940 to 1950, the Federal Reserve expanded the money supply and the growth of credit to enable the government to run budget deficits to pay for the costs of World War II. In the same period, the Federal Reserve capped the interest rate that they would pay on government securities to artificially keep interest rates low.

The 1970s' period was characterized by stagflation, the worst of all economic possibilities (except for outright depression).

In a stagflation economy, the economy grows slowly, and inflation is high. The stagflation of the 1970s was caused by the inept policies of the Federal government, the Federal Reserve expanding the money supply to counteract oil price shocks, and the de-linkage of the U.S. dollar from the gold standard.

During this period, Treasuries, bonds, and stocks did not do particularly well. In the beginning of the 1980s, inflation was rampant, running at a 12.4% annualized rate, the largest annual increase in inflation since the Civil War in 1860.

By the time Ronald Regan took office in 1982, inflation was spiraling out of control and Paul Volker, Chairman of the U.S. Federal Reserve, decided to halt inflation in its tracks.

Inflation was higher during the beginning of the 1980s than in the latter part of the decade. By 1989, it had dropped to 4.6%. Nonetheless, during the Regan administration, inflation was high again due to the expansion of the money supply and the growth in credit to finance the large defense expenditures that the government implemented.

During the 1990s, the Federal Reserve was moderate in expanding the money supply.

The Ebb and Flow of the Money Supply

When the Federal Reserve expands the money supply — usually to accommodate the bulging budget deficits — inflation rises. When the government makes a conscious effort to reduce the deficit and contracts the money supply (like President Clinton did between 1992 and 2000), inflation will be moderate. For example, inflation during Clinton's presidency averaged 2.3%.

Little or moderate inflation only occurs when the Federal Reserve contracts the money supply *and* the growth of credit, a rare occurrence.

Since we can never forecast the future with complete accuracy, we need to have diversified portfolios. For example, during periods when stocks are performing poorly, there is a likelihood that T-Bills or bonds will perform better.

The long-term performance of different asset classes can give us a realistic picture of how an asset class can perform over time.

Figure 5
Annual Total Returns — 1926 to 2003

Large Company Stocks	10.4%
Small Company Stocks	12.7%
Long-Term Corporate Bonds	5.9%
U.S. Treasury Bills	3.7%
Inflation	3.0%

Source: Ibbotson and Associates SBBI Yearbook

Risk and Unpredictable Markets

Markets have two cycles: up and down. Since none of us like pain, it's obvious we don't like declining markets. I get my fair share of concerned client calls when their monthly brokerage statements show a decline in one month. Many investors, unbelievably, don't understand that the market moves both ways. The people who try to sidestep declines by playing it safe generally miss any rally that ensues. It is better not to try to "time" the market, although there are plenty of market timing "gurus" out there who will argue differently.

> **"A wise man turns chance into good fortune"**
>
> –Thomas Fuller

Risk is multifaceted. There are asset class risks, economic, political, currency, and interest rate risks — and then there is company specific risk.

By diversifying into various asset classes, you can reduce your risk. For example, many investors tried to sidestep the decline in Southern California real estate between 1989 and 1995. However, many of these individuals missed the ensuing rally after 1995, one that is still going on, though it is showing signs of peaking. And that is when many of these people will be trying to buy back in — at the top.

Just remember: In the short term, any asset class can be

risky. A successful asset allocation plan will only work well if your timeframe is long enough, and you have patience. Don't be misled by others into thinking you will be successful in market timing. If you don't want to lose money then keep it in safe investments such as a money market account. Keep in mind, however, that you may not be able to accumulate enough assets on which to retire if you don't take some chances. The successful accumulation of wealth takes a long-term perspective.

There are times when asset classes can remain in the doldrums for significant periods. As an illustration, according to Lipper Analytical Services and The Institute for Business and Finance, stocks delivered a total return of 1.6% per year from December 1968 to December of 1978. Gold declined from $800 an ounce in 1982 and has never been above $475 an ounce since, which is why diversification in different assets is extremely important and critical to your financial future. You never know when one or more asset classes will perform well and when one or more asset classes will act badly. A properly diversified portfolio will smooth out the ups and downs of your investments.

Markets are inherently unpredictable and almost impossible to time. Only long-term investors who are well diversified have a chance of beating inflation, let alone arriving at a comfortable retirement.

Asset Class Risk

Asset class risk is "having too much of your money invested in any one class or sub-sector." It is important to diversify among at least the three major asset classes and within sub-sectors of each class.

For example, the S&P 500 as a class lost 43% of its value from March 8, 2000 to March 8, 2003, while bonds increased in value by over 20%. If you were invested in stocks alone, your portfolio would have dropped significantly.

Asset class risk can be mitigated in several ways, but a key point to remember is that you need to be patient, ride out short-term volatility, invest for the long-term, and be diversified.

Inflation Risk

Inflation risk is the loss of purchasing power over a period of time. It's a fact that purchased goods will cost more in the future than they do today, and if your assets do not keep up with inflation, there is a good chance you will run short of funds and have to reduce your lifestyle at some point.

According to the Institute of Business and Finance, consider the following:

- At 6.9% inflation, $1 dollar would lose over one-half of its purchasing power in 10 years.

- At 4% inflation, the same dollar would lose over half of its purchasing power in 20 years.

- At 5% inflation, you would need $105,000 in 40 years to buy a car that now costs $15,000.

Although volatility in markets is unpleasant and sometimes frightening, lowering one's living standards in the middle of retirement is much worse.

Therefore, as an intelligent and prudent individual, your investments must outpace inflation and taxes. The only way to do this is to compound your investments at a higher return than both inflation and taxes combined.

According to Ibbotson and Associates, short-term interest-bearing securities may keep up with inflation *some* of the time, but not always. For example, inflation was running at a 3.3% annual rate during 2003, and the 6- month U.S. Treasury Bill yielded 1.74% during the same period — a negative difference of -1.56%, that was before taxes. After taxes, short-term interest-bearing securities do not keep up with inflation.

Market Risk and Making Money from Volatility

Warren Buffett once stated that volatility can be an investor's friend because it provides "true" investors with the opportunity to purchase additional assets at a lower price, provided they like the asset in which they are invested.

All asset classes, except very short-term interest-bearing securities, are volatile. They fluctuate over time. However, it is also true that over time, most quality asset classes do generally move upward.

In Modern Portfolio Theory (MPT), there are measures of risk such as Standard Deviation (SD) and Beta. However, it is my opinion that risk, according to MPT, has not been adequately defined.

Risk needs to be separated into two distinct categories: market risk and financial risk. Beta and SD are attempts to quantify market risk and price uncertainty. Although Beta is a good indicator of price volatility, it is a poor indicator of uncertainty.

Current mathematical approaches to investing have put a considerable amount of emphasis on market fluctuations, but market price risk is not true risk because it is only risk associated with price fluctuations, not those associated with the business aspects of any particular company. Price volatility isn't risk associated with the financial structure of the company or with its prospects for the future.

Southern California Edison (SCE) — a utility that produces and sells electricity — and LSI Logic — a designer and manufacturer of computer chips — serve as prime examples of the fallacy of using Beta as a risk measurement tool.

During the past 10 years, SCE had an average Beta of .85 while LSI's average Beta was 1.50. Using the S&P 500 as a market benchmark, the Beta of the whole market would be 1. If a company like LSI Logic has a Beta of 1.50, then in general, this means if the market goes up, theoretically LSI should rise 50% more than the market. Conversely, if the market declines, then theoretically, LSI should decline 50% more than the market.

In SCE's case, with a Beta of .85, if the market rises, then SCE should rise 15% less than the market; and if the market declines, SCE should decline by less than 15%.

Using Beta as a risk measurement tool, one would think that SCE would be less risky than LSI, but this is not the case. As it turned out, SCE was far less stable and much riskier than LSI due to regulatory problems in California. Although SCE did not declare bankruptcy like its Northern California counterpart, Pacific Gas and Electric (PGE), it almost did and SCE suffered severe financial stress.

LSI Logic has experienced a downturn in its revenues because of the slowdown in technology spending, but it was in far better financial shape than either SCE or Pacific Gas, even though LSI has a higher Beta. Beta is simply not a practical and useful tool to properly evaluate risk.

If a company is poorly capitalized or experiences unfavorable regulation, the investor could be saddled with a riskier investment than a well-established company with excellent product lines and cash flow, even though the company has a higher Beta. Each case must be judged on its own merits.

The *true* indicator of risk is a function of *financial advantage* and is the difference between *intrinsic* value and *perceived* value. As stated previously, volatility in prices, while a bother to some, is not to others. Volatility can only be judged on an individual basis.

The gap between intrinsic (true) value and perceived (the value someone thinks an investment is worth) value is reduced as more and more traders enter the marketplace. The market price will move toward equilibrium and will come close to eliminating the price differential, but will never *completely* eliminate it. The market's true value and perceived value are entirely separate and, at times, a wide gap exists between the two different valuations.

During times of high market valuations, the gap between intrinsic and perceived values grows larger, and the risk of a large market decline increases. This is due to market forces narrowing the gap between intrinsic and perceived values. Stocks become expensively priced in relation to their earning power; but more importantly, the perception of value widens from what the true value actually is.

To illustrate: Much of a stock's price above book value is due to the investor's *perceived* future earning power of that security. Each investor has his own notion of what he is willing to pay for a security. This notion is based on his interpretation of the future earning power of that security.

Conversely, in times of undervaluation, the gap between intrinsic and perceived value is also wide, but in an opposite manner than when valuations are high. Stocks are priced much cheaper than they are truly worth. Again, this is due to the investor's perception of value.

In *Alchemy of Finance*, George Soros theorizes that the trader's gap is the difference between perception and reality.

Much of the time, the securities markets are almost in equilibrium. However, at other times, especially during periods of extreme euphoria or extreme pessimism, the markets become uncertain and quiet inefficient, swinging widely from one extreme to another.

The *perceptions* of traders move markets from overvaluation to undervaluation and back again. Sometimes these large swings are sudden, and sometimes it may take years for them to swing. However, in all markets, at some time or another, this phenomenon takes place and the investor can profit from it.

I have demonstrated that volatility can act in your favor if you have the temperament and the ability to understand and ride out volatile periods. Markets will swing back and forth, but if you can overcome your fear, you can profit from it.

For most people, however, overcoming this fear is very difficult. That notwithstanding, if you follow the models I discuss in this book, you stand a better chance of beating your trepidation because they offer an easier, more predictable path for investing.

One thing is clear: Traditional methods of calculating risk generally do not work, but a simple investment plan, followed in good and bad times, will most likely help you achieve your goal of a comfortable retirement.

Retirement Risk

Retirement risk is one peril that portfolio managers and academics never include in their risk analysis, but it is a very valid danger. Retirement risk is the threat that the retiree will run out of money before he passes away.

For many people, this threat is real, but unfortunately, most people never plan correctly for it.

For example, if your expenses run approximately $200,000 per year, using an investment return of 6% and a withdrawal rate of 4%, the investor will need approximately $5,000,000 in liquid assets [to draw out $200,000 per year from those assets].

How do your finances compare with this figure, and have you thought about your retirement risk rate? In order to avoid — or at least lessen — retirement risk, you will need to save more and invest wisely. Your asset base needs to support your retirement spending needs and to account for the ever-increasing inflation in our economy, as well as ongoing taxation.

The Different Asset Classes

Asset classes are simply a group of "like" investments. Bonds are an asset class and are distinctly different from an asset class such as stocks. To be properly diversified, you should have your investments spread over four asset classes that are not correlated with one another.

Correlation is a term used in statistics to determine how various assets or asset classes move in one direction or another relative to each other.

Diversified portfolios that are non-correlated do not move in tandem and do not move up or down together. A case in point: If you own a real estate investment trust (REIT) and an Exchange traded equity fund (ETF), you have a portfolio of two asset classes that are not correlated with one another.

> "Every time you think you've got the key to the market, some SOB changes the lock."
>
> –G. M. Loeb, quoted by Louis Rukeyser

The goal is to have enough asset classes that are non-correlated. If one asset class moves down, the other may move up. I've heard many stories from new clients who came to my firm in 2003, who believed that their financial advisor properly diversified their portfolio. However, after examining their brokerage statements, many showed that they had 20 stocks. These clients thought that by having 20 stocks they were diversified — they were not.

The problem was that, in most cases, many of the stocks were in the same industry, in these cases, technology. Yes, they were diversified if one company went out of business, but they were not diversified against a decline in one industry. Portfolios that had three or more distinct asset classes came through the 2000-2003 market decline with minimal losses.

One of the reasons these investors should have diversified their portfolios is that one asset or asset class may decline while another may increase. A diversified portfolio is less risky.

Gary Brinson, a Professor of Finance and Portfolio Manager, conducted a landmark study of asset class performance and found that approximately 90% of a portfolio's performance over time was due to the investor being invested in *that* asset class. To illustrate: The S&P 500 had a 12.99% return between 1984 and 2003. Ninety percent of the portfolio's performance could be attributed to the investor being in the S&P 500. By being invested in the S&P, an asset class, most of the return was due to simply being invested in large companies, companies which are part of the S&P.

Professor Roger Ibbotson, of Yale University, and Paul Kaplan, studied the same issue and confirmed the Brinson study results. Because of their findings and many of the rules I'm giving you, it is obvious and imperative that you diversify your portfolio to include at least three asset classes.

Figure 6
General Asset Class Groupings

Equities
Bonds
Cash
Real Estate
Precious Metals
Currencies
Commodities

Figure 7
General Sub-Asset Class Groupings

Large-capitalization growth
Large-capitalization value
Small-capitalization growth
Small-capitalization value
International
Emerging markets
Mid-capitalization growth
Mid-capitalization value
Investment grade bonds
Junk bonds
Government securities
Tax-free bonds
Corporate bonds
Foreign bonds
Venture capital
Gold
Silver
Timber
REITS

The asset classes in Figure 6 are *general* in nature, while the asset classes in Figure 7 are subclasses. To be truly diversified, you need to be invested in at least three general asset classes and further diversified in sub-classes.

There are a multitude of recommendations made by advisors and other pundits. The truth is that there is no individual choice that is perfect. Choices can only be suggestive, and asset allocation is up to each investor.

Building upon the Brinson and Ibbotson studies, Dr. William Bernstein, author of *The Intelligent Asset Allocator*, has a useful method to determine an investor's asset allocation. For example, instead of an investor choosing an asset allocation of 50% stocks, the investor decides how much risk he would be able to tolerate. The exposure of equities would determine the volatility of the portfolio. Dr. Bernstein's table is reproduced below as Figure 8.

Figure 8
Asset Allocation Based on Risk Preference

I can tolerate losing __% of my portfolio in the course of earning higher returns	Recommend % of portfolio in stocks
35%	80%
30%	70%
25%	60%
20%	50%
15%	40%
10%	30%
5%	20%
0%	10%

Source: The Intelligent Asset Allocator

As an advisor, when I meet new clients and discuss their tolerance for risk, I ask the client, "How much could your portfolio decline without you losing any sleep?" If the answer is 15%, then I know, using Bernstein's table, that this particular client's asset allocation to stocks should not be more than 40%. If they can stand to lose 20%, then I know to limit their equity exposure to 50%. What is your sleeping point?

A person's background has a lot to do with how they view risk and how much they can tolerate. An individual who is highly averse to risk and, for most of his life, has invested in secure interest-paying securities (e.g., Money Markets, Certificates of Deposit) would not be a good candidate for a large stock portfolio.

When the market declines as it does, that person would not be able to stay the course. In other words, he would not be able to sleep at night. No matter what an advisor tells him about being invested in stocks for the long- term or how much the investor reads about the stock market, he will be going against his basic instincts; and he will either be miserable or pull his money out of the market at precisely the wrong time.

I had a client who went against his nature and lost. Larry avoided the stock market when it was going strong and felt left out when he heard that his friends were making a lot of money. He had been a CD investor his whole life, but typical of the herd mentality, he jumped in right at the top of the market in 1999. He sold out in 2001, precisely at the bottom of the market. Larry simply could not withstand the psychological pain of watching his portfolio decline.

Some people want to make great returns but don't want to take the risk to enjoy them. One of the fundamental rules of Modern Portfolio Theory is that the larger risk an investor takes, the larger the return he will receive. I have never seen this fundamental rule violated.

Harriet, a potential client, walked into my office in late 1999, told me how much her friends were making in the technology sector of the market, and said that she wanted in as well, expecting a 25% annual return.

I explained to her the fundamental rules of risk and return and told her if she wanted that kind of return — which I did not think was possible on a long-term basis — she would have to take an extraordinary amount of risk.

She replied, "But I don't want to take any risk."

As you can imagine, I did not want Harriet as a client. Most people don't understand the basic concept of risk and return, and they certainly don't understand that their investments must be in line with their pain tolerance.

Sometimes, investors evolve, especially if they understand the markets. When I was still in college, I was pretty risk averse and hesitant to put a lot of money in the stock market. However, as I became educated and learned about business, economics, and investing, I became much less risk averse.

Value versus Growth

Since I understand the risk reward rules and I practice the art and science of Security Analysis, I now feel comfortable in having a large exposure of my total net worth in the stock market. However, even my psychology has limits. For example, I invest in value stocks and employ the philosophies of the late Benjamin Graham. Although I have evolved somewhat, I am still a true value investor. My psychology would not permit me to be a growth investor because I view it as too risky. If a growth stock misses its earnings estimates, the investment community will pummel the stock, and it could decline by over 20% in one week.

Omnicare is a good case in point. Omnicare was a pharmacy benefits company that reported one-quarter of poor earnings when their stock declined from 41 to 27 in one week. This kind of volatility does not suit my personality. Every time I've ventured into risky assets, I paid the price in lost sleep and money, and I always come crawling back to my value roots.

Other investors are risk takers and want an aggressive investment program — their personalities permit them to do it. However, as we will see, value investors nearly always outperform *growth* investors.

Growth and value investors are constantly battling it out to see which style performs better. Morningstar-style boxes delineate investment styles between growth and value, large, mid-cap, and small capitalization stocks. The Morningstar-style box is very useful in determining if a fund is a growth fund or a value fund and it can be helpful in determining style drift. (Style drift is when a fund *says* it is a value fund, but is in truth, a growth fund.) For example, Legg Mason Value Trust claims to be a value fund, but in my opinion, it is actually a mixture of growth and value.

When Bill Miller, Value Trust's Portfolio Manager, was asked to explain why he thought Amazon.com was a value stock, he replied, "Value is relative." Regardless of the style, Bill Miller has an exceptional performance record.

Value *is* relative, but only to a certain degree. Morningstar helps the fund investor determine exactly what style of fund he has, or is interested in.

In general, growth stocks have some defining characteristics. They have high-price-to-earnings ratios, high rates of growth in earnings and revenues, and high-price-to-book ratios.

In contrast, value stocks have low PE ratios, slower growth in earnings and revenues, and low-price-to-book ratio. Growth stocks are fast growing companies with large increases in sales, sometimes with earnings, while value stocks usually have slower increases in sales and earnings. Another reason a growth stock can become a value stock is for some reason or another the market has fallen out with it. Figure 9 below illustrates some common characteristics of growth and value stocks.

Figure 9
Growth and Value Stocks: Common Characteristics

Growth

PE	Price to book	Quarterly earnings growth	Quarterly earnings growth	Div. yield
<20	<4	<20	<20	0%

Value

>15	>2	>10	>10	<3%

> = *Lower than*
< = *Higher than*

Value Is a Better Proposition

Value stocks are often turnaround situations or companies that have had some disappointing news. They are of value for one reason or another. Some academics view them as riskier than growth stocks for the reasons outlined above. In my opinion, growth stocks for the reasons outlined above. In my opinion, this is nonsense; and as Benjamin Graham and others have repeatedly pointed out and confirmed by performance and other risk measures, value is *less* risky and provides better performance. Why is that? It is precisely because value stocks are shunned by the markets, in most cases temporarily; and that for the most part, they usually recover.

The herd usually follows the same direction for equities and because they do, they shun value stocks instead of waiting and being patient for the company to turn around. This provides a fertile ground for those groomed in Graham's methods of security analysis to determine if the operating characteristics of a company are generally sound and if the misfortune or bad news is permanent or temporary. If the company is sound and has a solid business, and the bad news is temporary, the enterprising security analyst will have found a bargain from which he or she can profit handsomely.

Benjamin Graham, Warren Buffett, and Mario Gabelli, to name just a few, are well-known value investors who have profited nicely from using this approach.

Benjamin Graham's *Security Analysis* is the investment philosophy that I use at my firm and what I teach at UCLA. I know my clients, my students, and I have profited heavily from using a value approach.

Eugene Fama, a professor from the University of Chicago, studied the performances of different styles of investing and concluded that the value style was superior to growth. Roger Ibbotson conducted a similar study that came to the same conclusion: In terms of performance, value is superior to growth over long periods.

Using data from Ibbotson and Associates *Stocks, Bonds, Bills, and Inflation Yearbook*, we conclude that over periods of time (1969-2003), value stocks enjoyed better performance than growth stocks with less risk

Figure 10
**Annual Total Returns of Value and Growth Stocks
1969-2003**

	Arithmetic Mean (%)	Standard Deviation (%)
Large Capitalization Growth	11.3	20.6
Large Capitalization Value	12.3	17
Mid Capitalization Growth	12	22.1
Mid Capitalization Value	15.5	19.7
Small Capitalization Growth	12.1	25.2
Small Capitalization Value	17.3	22
All Growth Stocks	11.2	20.2
All Value Stocks	12.9	17.2

Source: Ibbotson Associates SBBI 2003 yearbook

As we can see from Figure 10 above, all value stocks had an arithmetic performance between 1969 and 2003 of 12.9% versus the all growth stock portfolio of 11.2%. The difference of 1.17% may not seem large, but over time, this difference is significant.

If an investor had $1,000,000 invested over a 20-year period, the 1.17% in reduced performance would amount to over $130,000. The investor could have had better performance with less risk. The investor in small capitalization value stocks could have gotten a 17.3% return, which was significantly better than the performance of either mid-capitalization or large-capitalization stocks. However, the standard deviation was a relatively high 22%, which is more than the U.S. stock market standard deviation of approximately 20%. In any case, an intelligent investor who has a diversified portfolio would not have a portfolio consisting of all small-capitalization value stocks because it would be too risky.

Although some may dispute that value is superior to growth, it is clear that using a value investing philosophy produces better performance results with less risk than using a growth approach. I have advocated using the value approach throughout my entire investing career as a professional portfolio manager and security analyst.

Determining what kind of investor you are

The question we return to is: What type of investor are you? The following statements will help you determine if you are a conservative, moderate, or aggressive investor. Some statements are applicable to all investor types and as such may appear in each.

> "To be or not to be—that is the question."
>
> –William Shakespeare

Ask Yourself These Simple Questions

1.   I am more concerned about protecting my assets than about growth.
2.   I prefer the ease of mutual funds to the uncertainty of trying to pick winning stocks.
3.   Professional advisors and mutual funds may achieve higher growth than I can.
4.   I am comfortable with investments that promise slow, long-term appreciation and growth.
5.   I don't brood over bad investment decisions I have made.
6.   I feel comfortable with aggressive growth investments.
7.   I don't like surprises.
8.   My immediate concern is for income rather than growth opportunities.

9. I am a risk taker.
10. I make investment decisions comfortably and quickly.
11. I like predictability and routine in my daily life.
12. I usually pick the tried and true, the slow and safe but sure investments.
13. I need to focus my investment efforts on reserve funds and insurance rather than growth.
14. I prefer predictable, steady returns on my investments, even if the return is low.

Source: Silverplanner by Moneytree Software

If you answered yes to three or more of the following statements, you are most likely a conservative investor.

1. I am more concerned about protecting my assets than about growth.
2. I don't like surprises.
3. My immediate concern is for income rather than growth opportunities.
4. I like predictability and routine in my daily life.
5. I need to focus my investment efforts on reserve funds and insurance rather than growth.
6. I prefer predictable, steady returns on my investments, even if the returns are low.

If you answered yes to three or more of the statements you are most likely a moderate investor.

1. I prefer the ease of mutual funds to the uncertainty of trying to pick winning stocks.
2. I am comfortable with investments that promise slow, long-term appreciation and growth.
3. I don't brood over bad investment decisions I have made.
4. I am optimistic about my financial future.

5.   I usually pick the tried and true, the slow and safe but sure investments.
6.   Professional advisors and mutual funds may achieve higher growth than I can.

If you answered yes to three or more of the following statements, you are most likely an aggressive investor.

1.   Professional advisors and mutual funds most likely achieve lower growth than I can.
2.   I don't brood over bad investment decisions I have made.
3.   I feel comfortable with aggressive growth investments.
4.   I am a risk taker.
5.   I make investment decisions comfortably and quickly.

Computerized Asset Allocation Analyzers

As useful as these investor types are, they don't take into consideration some very important factors. If your goal is a well-funded retirement, then you have several choices on which to build up your asset base. You could be very lucky and inherit a lot of money. Or you can save a lot of your earnings; however, most people build a retirement nest by saving and investing well. In order to reduce the amount of money a retiree needs to save for his retirement, the rate of return on his investments needs to be substantial enough to make his savings grow. I have developed special asset allocation calculators on my Web site — **www.stevensfirstprinciples.com** — that take into account different planning variables. On the left scrollbar, go to the bottom and click on calculators. Once you are on the page entitled "Financial Calculators," look for the asset calculator. I have calculated the results for a person 51 years of age and have shown the results in Figure 10 below, using various assumptions.

Figure 11
Asset Allocation Calculator

Definitions
Age
Your current age. This is by far the most important aspect of asset allocation. For most people, the majority of their portfolio is for their retirement. The younger you are, the less likely you need this money any time soon, which allows you to invest more aggressively in stocks that generally have the best long-term returns. As you get older, it is advisable to move more of your investments to securities with less fluctuation, such as cash and bonds. This can help ensure that the money is available when you need it.

Current assets
This is the total value of your investment portfolio. Our asset allocator increases your stock exposure as your portfolio increases. Generally speaking, larger portfolios are less likely to leave individuals cash poor in a market downturn, which allows people with large portfolios to invest a bit more aggressively.

Savings per year
You will be adding this amount to your investments each year. Like portfolio size, the more you invest the more aggressive your investments should be.

Income required
This is the percentage of income you will need from your investments. Most people do not require any income from their investments until they retire.

Marginal tax rate
The tax rate you expect to pay on your investments.

Risk tolerance

Your personal ability to tolerate your portfolio value fluc-
tuating up and down. Many people overestimate their ability to tolerate risk. Unless you can handle a 20% decline in
your portfolio during a stock market correction, you may
wish to keep your risk tolerance at or below the mid-point.

Economic outlook

This is your view of future economic growth and the over-
all health of the economy. The better your outlook, the
more aggressive you can be with your investments.

Age	51
Current assets	$500,000+
Savings per year	$20,000+
Income required	4%+
Marginal tax rate	27%
Risk tolerance	7 (scale of 0 to 10)
Economic outlook	5 (scale of 0 to 10)

Suggested Asset Allocation		
Large cap stock	16%	$81,433
Mid cap stock	18%	$90,756
Small cap stock	15%	$76,385
Foreign stock	21%	$101,185
Bonds	12%	$62,233
Municipal bonds	10%	$48,493
Cash	8%	$39,515

No calculator, "rule-of-thumb," or chart will be perfect, nor will
it be suitable for every circumstance. Every asset allocation is an
individual choice and must factor in risk tolerance and investment goals.

In order to reach your investment goal and to have enough
funds for retirement, you will need to balance your fear of risk
with your need to achieve a certain rate of return on your

investments. Reward goes hand-in-hand with risk and for you to achieve your goal, you might need to take at least a moderate amount of risk.

11

Five Model Portfolios for the Investor

Once you have determined what assets you have and in what classes, then the process of redistribution to the targeted asset classes may begin. However, if you have significant assets that are illiquid, such as real estate, you may choose to wait for an opportunity to redistribute the assets in a more balanced fashion.

Even for the seasoned investor, the path to financial success is not always clear. The answer lies within the investor, and it depends on his or her appetite for — or aversion to — risk. The investment also depends on the investor's age, financial resources, and timeframe. However, for these purposes, I have laid out a basic framework to help you refine your decisions.

> "Any dammed fool can write a plan. It's the execution that gets you all screwed up."
>
> –James F. Hollingsworth, On Strategy: A Critical Analysis of the Vietnam War

First, you have to start. Many people don't have any money to invest, or they are afraid to take any chances. In the case of not having any money to invest, it's obvious you simply have to save as much as possible and cut expenditures.

If you have little savings, then the first step is to make a plan to save at least 10% to 15% of your gross income. A good way to start is to buy U.S. Savings Bonds, which I discuss in Chapter 12. Your employer can arrange to have some money deducted from your paycheck to pay for the bonds. Since you won't see the money, you won't miss it as much.

For those who have a desire and the discipline, plan to save the same 10% to 15% of your gross savings.

In Chapter 10, I briefly listed some general asset classes. The following is a more comprehensive listing of the primary asset classes and sub-asset classes.

Figure 12
Comprehensive Primary Asset Classes

Interest-bearing Securities
Equities
Commodities
Real Estate

Figure 13
Comprehensive Sub-Asset Classes for Interest-bearing Securities

Corporate Bonds	U.S. Treasury Notes
Convertible Bonds	U.S. Treasury Bonds
Bankers Acceptance	TIPS
Preferred Stocks	Tax-free Issues
Money Market Accounts	U.S. Agency Notes
Convertible Bonds	Exchange Traded Funds
ConvertiblePreferred Stocks	Bond Index Funds
Bank Certificate of Deposit	High Yield (Junk)
U.S. Treasury Bills	Sovereign Debt
Commercial Paper	Foreign Bonds

Figure 14
Comprehensive Sub-Asset Class for Equities

Domestic Equities small capitalization growth
International Equities
Domestic Equities mid capitalization growth

Emerging Equities
Domestic Equities large capitalization growth
Exchange Traded Funds
Open-end Index Funds
Domestic Equities small capitalization value
Private Equity
Venture Capital
Domestic Equities mid capitalization value

Figure 15
Comprehensive Sub-Asset Class for Real Estate

Real Estate Investment Trusts   (REITS)
REIT Exchange Traded Funds
REIT Open-end Index Funds
Residence
Vacation Property
Investment Property
Timberland
Farmland

Figure 16
Comprehensive Sub-Asset Class for Commodities

Commodity Index Funds
Precious Metals
Commodity Futures
Gold
Silver
Gold Equities
Silver Equities
Closed-end Silver/Gold Fund (CEF)
Gold Open-end Mutual Funds
Oil Equities
Exchange Traded Natural Resources Fund
Coal Equities

The Simplified Plan Models

Note: All of the illustrated models are suited for long-term investing and not meant for speculators and/or market timers. I have used Exchange traded funds (ETF) because their expense ratios are low. In some cases I have used Vanguard Index Funds because their expense ratios are low as well. I explain what Exchange traded funds and mutual funds are in Chapter 14.

Model One:
The Conservative Investor

This model is designed for those who are not comfortable with risk. As we saw in Chapter 9, risk comes in various forms. An investment plan that is too conservative will lower market risks but could possibly increase inflation or retirement risk. Therefore, the conservative investor needs to constantly evaluate to determine if Model One is not outpacing inflation and the chances of the investor not meeting his or her goal.

Investors who are retired — or those who do not want to have a large exposure in real estate, commodities, precious metals, and equities — can use Model One. Examples of conservative investors would be a widow, an invalid, and a person in their late 50s or early 60s, or one who doesn't want too much risk.

Primary Asset Class: Interest Bearing Securities	70%
Sub-Asset Class TIPS Treasury Inflation Protection Securities (TIPS) Individual TIPS with maturities less than 10 years OR Vanguard TIP Fund Symbol: (VIPSX)	35%
Sub-Asset Class U.S. Treasuries U.S. Treasury Notes and Bills Laddered Portfolio 1, 2, 3, 4, 5 years OR	30%

1/2 Lehman Brothers ETF Symbol: (SHY)
AND
1/2 Vanguard Intermediate U.S. Treasury Portfolio Symbol: (VIPSX)

Sub-Asset Class   Corporate Bonds   5%
Goldman Sachs ETF Corp Bonds Symbol (LQD)
OR
Vanguard Corporate Bond Fund, Symbol: (VBIX)

Asset Class   Real Estate   5%

Sub-Asset Class   REITS
Real Estate Investment Trust ETF Symbol: (IYR)
OR
Vanguard Real Estate Index Symbol: (VGSIX)

Asset Class   Equities   25%

Sub-Asset Class   Domestic Equities: 15%
Russell 3000 Value ETF Symbol (IWW)
OR
Vanguard Extended Market Index Symbol: (VTSMX)

Sub-Asset Class   International Equities   10%
ETF Symbol (EFA)
OR
Vanguard International Index Fund Symbol: (VGTSX)

Model Two:
The Moderate Investor

An investor who wants capital appreciation and preservation can use this model. The moderate investor model is well-suited for the long-term investor. In this model, less interest-bearing securities are being utilized with an increase in equities, real estate, and commodities. The model for a moderate individual would be someone who wants a measured amount of risk; for example, an investor in his or her late 40s or early 50s.

Primary Asset Class   Equities   35%

Sub-Asset Class   Domestic Equities   25%
Russell 3000 Value ETF Symbol (IWW)

Sub-Asset Class   International Equities   5%
ETF Symbol (EFA)
OR
Vanguard International Index Symbol: (VGTSX)

Sub-Asset Class   Emerging Markets   5%
ETF Symbol: (EEM)

Primary Asset Class   Real Estate*   10%

Sub-Asset Class   REITS
ETF Real Estate Symbol: (IYR)
OR
Vanguard Real Estate Index Fund Symbol: (VGSIX)

Primary Asset Class   Commodities   5%
Pimco Real Commodity Index Fund (PCRDX)

Primary Asset Class   Interest-bearing

Sub-Asset Class   TIPS   35%
TIPS
OR
Vanguard TIP Fund Symbol: (VIPSX)

Sub-Asset Class   Tax Free Issues   10%
Tax-Free Individual Issues
OR

Vanguard Tax-Free Intermediate Bond Portfolio

(Please note that the proper bond portfolio depends on your state of residence. Go to **www.vanguard.com** *for details.)*

Sub-Asset Class	Treasuries	5%

U.S. Treasury Bills (6 month)

* Note that real estate allocations would be zero if your residence or other real estate were more than 10% of the total assets on your personal balance sheet.

Model Three:
The Aggressive Investor

The model for the aggressive investor is designed for those individuals who can tolerate a fair degree of volatility, a loss in a short to intermediate period of time, and/or is in the rapid accumulation phase of his financial life. For example, an aggressive individual might be in his 20s or 30s or is risk tolerant and desires an aggressive approach.

Primary Asset Class	Equities	50%

Sub-Asset Class	Domestic Equities	35%

Russell 3000 Value ETF Symbol (IWW)
OR
Vanguard Total Market Index (VTSMX)

Sub-Asset Class	International Equities	10%

ETF Symbol (EFA) OR Vanguard International
Index Fund Symbol (VGTSX)

Sub-Asset Class	Emerging Markets	5%

ETF Symbol (EEM) OR Vanguard
Emerging Market Fund Symbol (VEIEX)

Primary Asset Class	Real Estate	10%

Residence, Investment Properties
OR
ETF Symbol (IYR)
OR
Vanguard REIT Index Symbol (VGSIX)

Primary Asset Class	Commodities 1	10%

ETF Goldman Sachs Natural Resources Symbol (IGE)	5%
Pimco Real Commodity Fund (PCRDX)	5%

Primary Asset Class	Interest-bearing Securities	30%

Sub-Asset Class	TIPS	20%

Individual TIPS
OR
Vanguard TIP fund Symbol: (VIPSX)

Sub-Asset Class	Treasuries	10%

Model Four: Inflation Model

Inflation is an inherent part of the world's fiat currency system as it stands now. Governments have encouraged inflation since the true gold standard was abandoned after World War 1. Since excessive money and credit creation fuel inflation, it is unlikely that the governments of the world will eliminate inflation altogether. In addition, it is quite possible that inflation will accelerate greatly in the coming years.

Although a hyperinflation in the United States is unlikely, a moderate inflation over time can inflict a lot of damage as well. To address this possibility, I have developed an inflation model.

Since long-term economic forecasting and predictions are highly suspect, the Inflation Model is well-suited for speculators.

It is important to note that if a high rate of inflation does not happen, the inflation portfolio model should be redistributed into one of the other three investment models previously outlined. Inflation has averaged approximately 4% over the past 50 years.

Primary Asset Class	Real Estate	25%

Residential Real Estate, Investment Properties,
Farmland, Timber, ETF REIT Index (IYR),
OR
Vanguard REIT Index (VGSIX), Plum Creek Timber
REIT (PCL), and Rayonier Timber REIT Symbol (RYN)

Primary Asset Class	Commodities	10%

Pimco Real Commodity Fund (PCRDX)	5%
ETF Goldman Sachs Natural Resources	
Fund Symbol (IGE)	5%

Sub-Asset Class	Gold/Silver	10%
ETF Gold Exchange Traded Fund Symbol (CLGLF.PK)		5%
Central Fund Canada Closed-end Fund Symbol (CEF)		5%

Asset Class	Interest-bearing Securities	55%

Sub-Asset Class	TIPS	35%

Individual TIPS, I Savings Bonds
OR
Vanguard TIPS Fund Symbol (VIPSX)

Sub-Asset Class	U.S Treasuries	20%

6-month Treasury Bills

A Note about Inflation: I have used Individual TIPS or the Vanguard TIP fund because of liquidity. An investor could substitute TIPS or Vanguard's TIP fund for U.S. Savings Bonds, Series I. However, I-

Bonds have a 30-year maturity; we have suggested a duration of 6 years for all bonds and a duration of no more than 10 for TIPS.

The advantage of I-Bonds is that the tax on the interest is deferred until the investor cashes in the bond, while TIP investors in individual issues pay tax on the imputed TIP interest ever year even though the interest isn't received until maturity. Current U.S. Treasury regulations prohibit any one person from buying more than $33,000 of I-Bonds per year. A couple can purchase $66,000, and a trust can purchase $33,000.

Another consideration before investing in U.S. Treasuries or TIPS is the fact that because of federal budget pressures, including Medicare and Social Security, the United States Government could default on its obligations. This has happened before. In the American Revolution, the newly-formed United States Government printed money called Continental dollars, without any backing, to pay for the revolutionary war — hence the term, "Not worth a continental."

During the American Civil War, the same thing happened, but with "Greenbacks." The government simply printed dollars in green without any backing, and inflation ensued.

Today, the U.S. Government does things differently by issuing Treasury securities to borrow money instead of just blatantly printing money. Therefore, there is an enormous amount of debt in the world markets which, in all likelihood, won't be paid back in full. Instead of outright default, which could happen, it is more likely that the government will cause a wholesale inflation to ensue.

Experience in many other countries, especially Germany after World War I, serve as good examples. In the case of outright default or wholesale inflation, the best investment path would not be in bonds but rather in commodities such as gold or hard assets such as real estate. Although stocks are an imperfect hedge against inflation, they will hold more value than bonds.

Again, Germany serves as an example after World War I, according to Benjamin Graham in The Intelligent Investor: "Those investors who held bonds, government or corporate, were completely wiped out, while those investors who owned stocks, lost 92% of the value of their money. The investors who held stocks saw a significant decline in the value of their money, but they were not totally wiped out like bond investors.

However, the markets eventually recovered and while the bond investors never did, most of the stock investors recovered their money."

Though real estate serves as a good hedge against inflation, home prices generally do not. Unbelievably, the long-term rate of return on residential real estate has been 2% over the rate of inflation. For example, if the long-term rate of inflation has been 4% from 1926 through 2003, then residential real estate has produced a real return of 2% to 3% over inflation; or roughly, 6% to 7%. According to an article in the Wall Street Journal, residential real estate, adjusted for inflation, has produced a 6% return, which is far worse than the stock market.

Inflation has accelerated since the 1970s, and the rate of return on real estate may be higher because of it. Regardless, residential real estate should be part of everyone's portfolio, but in the form of actually living in it. Most people would be better off placing their real estate investments in professionally managed Real Estate Investment Trusts (REITS). Why? Because they are professionally managed, and they pay great dividends, usually averaging 5% or more. However, if the investor has the time, ability, and knowledge, then owning real estate directly is a good inflation hedge.

In inflationary times, increase the amount of money in real estate, timber, gold, and silver, and possibly in currencies other than the U.S. dollar.

It is quite possible that the U.S. equities markets will be entering a period of low returns. According to BCA Research (**www.bcaresearch.com**), U.S. equity fundamentals are pointing to a period of low returns, averaging 4% to 8% per year, far below what the market has experienced since 1982 when the bull market began.

There are good reasons for this dire prediction. For one, the S&P 500 delivered a real compound rate of return, 15% annualized from 1982 to 2000, while U.S. Treasury Bonds had a real return of 9%.

According to BCA and Ibbottson Associates, the above performance figures are compared to the long-term performance average return of 5.3% annualized return for stocks and less than a 1% return for bonds in the past 100 years.

The market experienced a lengthy period in which returns were above normal. The market now has to enter a period of below normal performance to revert to what should be long-term performance averages for stocks and bonds. This is what is referred to as "regressing to the mean."

What fueled this "out" performance? There are three reasons. First, for over a decade (1969-1982), the global equity market had experienced sub-performance. Second, interest rates dropped from 13% in 1982 to 5.5% in 2000. Third, PE ratios, in general, expanded from a low of 8 in 1982 to over 25 in 2000.

Now we have the opposite scenario. Interest rates are increasing from 2% in 2004, the PE is shrinking, and we had a decade of out-performance.

The Gordon Model is a useful tool to determine future U.S. equity returns.

Figure 17
The Gordon Model

The Gordon Model is simply:
S&P 500 growth rate in earnings + dividend = Stock market return (annualized)
For example, if the S&P 500 is projected to grow its earnings 5% and the dividend yield of the S&P is 1.7%, then the S&P should deliver a 6.7% annualized return.

Figure 18
Growth Rate Using Gordon Model

S&P Earnings Growth Rate = 5%
S&P 500 Dividend Yield = 1.7%
5% + 1.7% = 6.7% projected annualized return of the S&P

If we believe that the Gordon Model is predictive of future stock market returns, it is highly likely that the U.S. stock market will return between 6% and 7% on an annualized basis.

If, for some reason, the PE multiple continues to expand and/or S&P earnings increase above 5%, then the stock market could possibly deliver a higher return. However, that is unlikely because in order for the S&P to deliver a higher growth rate in earnings, the United States Gross Domestic Product (GDP) would have to grow at a higher rate than in the past, or at what is sustainable.

The United States GDP can comfortably grow at a real 3%. If you add 3% (a minimum figure) for inflation, then the growth rate in S&P earnings would be 6% (3% GDP + 3% inflation). If inflation runs at 4%, then the S&P could grow at 7%. If you want to know what the average sustainable growth in S&P 500 earnings are, simply add GDP growth rate in percent and the inflation rate.

Bonds will probably not deliver large out-sized returns either. If the long-term equilibrium rate of interest is 5% and inflation is 2%, then the real rate of return on long-term U.S. Treasuries will be 3%. The real rate of return for bonds is simply the nominal or stated rate of return minus the inflation rate (5% — 2% = 3%). If the equilibrium rate of return on the 10- year U.S. Treasury Bond is 5% and inflation is 4%, then the real return on the 10-year bond is 1% (or not much of a return at all).

The real rate of return is always the nominal interest (i.e., the stated interest rate as reported in the financial press) minus the inflation rate, which is the real interest rate return that bonds produce. Comparing returns using the real rate tells you how your investments have performed.

Although fully aware of the error in forecasting far into the future, I have nonetheless developed a model for a low return environment for this type of situation.

Since forecasting is extremely difficult — and the chances of being right are as good as the chances of being wrong — the safer route is to adopt Model Two for the moderate investor.

In the unlikely event that the United States experiences a severe deflation, I have developed a deflation investment model that is well suited for returns in a low return environment that we may be experiencing now. Although I don't believe we are on the cusp of a deflation, the U.S. may experience low returns for the next several years because of markets regressing to the mean.

Model Five:
Deflation or Low Return Model

Primary Asset Class Equities	40%

Sub-Asset Class Domestic Equities	
I-shares Dividend Index Fund ETF Symbol (DVY)	10%
John Hancock Patriot Dividend Closed-end Fund Symbol (DIV)	10%
ETF Utility Fund Symbol (IDU)	5%
Russell 3000 Value ETF Symbol (IWW)	5%

Sub-Asset Class Emerging markets	5%
ETF Emerging Market Index Fund (EEM)	

Sub-Asset Class International Equities	5%
Aberdeen Global Income Closed-end Fund Symbol (FCO)	5%

Primary Asset Class Real Estate	10%

Sub-Asset Class REITS	10%

Primary Asset Class Commodities	10%
ETF Goldman Sachs Natural Resources Symbol (IGE)	5%
Pimco Real Commodity Fund Symbol (PCRDX)	5%

Primary Asset Class Interest-bearing Securities	40%

Sub-Asset Class TIPS	10%
Individual TIPS	
OR	
Vanguard TIP fund Symbol (VIPSX)	
Sub-Asset Class Treasuries	20%

Ladder 6-month, 1, 2 year
OR
ETF Treasury Fund (SHY)

Sub-Asset Class   Tax Free Issues   10%
Individual Tax-Free Issues
AND/OR
Nuveen Municipal Closed-end Fund (NUV)

Useful Working Guidelines to Determine Valuation

Obviously, it's best to invest when markets for the particular securities you are going to purchase are not overvalued. Although there is no perfect gauge of overvaluation or undervaluation, there are some useful guidelines. Benjamin Graham spent his entire career trying to devise a way to tell if the stock market was overvalued or undervalued, and he never was successful.

Useful Working Guidelines for the U.S. Stock Market

- The U.S. Stock Market is very undervalued when the average PE is below 10.
- The U.S. Stock Market is generally undervalued when the average Dividend Yield is above 4%.
- The U.S. Stock Market is generally undervalued when the EP ratio (earnings divided by price) is 3% to 5% over the 6-month U.S. Treasury Bill.
- The U.S. Stock Market is at fair value when the PE Ratio of the general market is 13.
- The U.S. Stock Market is at fair value when the Dividend Yield of the general market is around 3%.
- The U.S. Stock Market is overvalued when the PE Ratio is above 17.
- The U.S. Stock Market is overvalued when the dividend yield is below 2.5%.

- The U.S. Stock Market is overvalued when the EP ratio is 3% and below.

With commodities and real estate, there are no real gauges of valuation except in commercial real estate, which is a specialized business. In commercial real estate, the capitalization rate (cap rate) is used to determine proper levels of valuation.

If you own real estate (and it seems speculation in real estate has gone wild), be prepared to hold the property for a long period (at least 10 years or more with residential property) before you take your profits. Speculation is not for the timid.

Timing the market is extremely difficult, if not impossible, to do; and timing is always uncertain. It is best to broadly diversify your portfolio — using my suggested models — and spread your risk than to attempt to time either the stock market or real estate.

12 Interest Bearing Investments

This book has been about developing a simple investment plan. In general, it is much simpler to reach your goals through a plan that allocates your money using funds. However, when it comes to interest-bearing securities, in my opinion, it is far better to own individual securities.

The advantage of owning individual securities is that you can hold them until they mature. If interest rates rise and you have a loss in bonds, you can always hold them until maturity. If you do so, you will not lose any of your principal.

The opposite is true if you have interest-bearing securities in funds. Since the fund is always buying and selling securities, they do not hold their investments until maturity. Many bond investors in funds found that they faced large losses in 1994 when their bond funds declined by 20%, and in 2003 when some funds dropped as much as 15%.

One problem in owning individual securities, especially if you've invested less than $150,000, is the lack of diversification. Diversification in bonds is as important as it is in stocks. If the amount of money you have to invest is less than $150,000, then you should use funds, except for U.S. obligations. Interest-bearing securities issued by the U.S. Treasury and U.S. Agencies are

> "More people get killed chasing after a higher yield than looking down the barrel of a gun."
>
> –William LeFevre

very safe. U.S. Treasuries have the full faith and credit of the U.S. Government, and the government will not default on those obligations (hopefully!).

In the extremely unlikely scenario that this country were to become financially unstable, the U.S. Government would simply print more money or raise taxes to pay the principal and interest on its obligations. If it came to that point, most other investments except gold, commodities, and land would be practically worthless. The risk of default on U.S. Agency interest-bearing securities is small. However, they are not guaranteed by the full faith and credit of the United States Government, as are T-Bills.

However, I doubt that the politicians in Washington, D.C., would let any agency default on its debt. Instead, the result would be a Congressional bailout. Remember, politicians want your vote and they want to remain in office as long as possible.

Diversification is important with tax-free issues and extremely important with corporate bonds. Funds are good choices in certain circumstances, if you don't have enough money to diversify in individual issues.

To have a properly diversified bond portfolio outside of U.S. Government issues, you should have a minimum of 20 different bonds in a minimum denomination of $15,000 in each issue, especially if your asset class selection is corporate bonds.

Tax-free issues, if insured by an outside carrier such as AMBAC or MBIA, pose little risk in terms of default, although they are subject to interest rate and inflation risk, as are other bonds. However, corporate bonds are a different story because they are subject to credit — as well as interest and inflation — risks. Corporate bonds can be highly rated one day and then their ratings can suddenly plummet, causing your investment to go from investment grade to junk status.

Bond Basics

Success with corporate bonds requires the same kind of in-depth analysis that stock choices demand. This analysis is time-consuming and can be tricky. Corporations can use ingenious ways to disguise their earnings and hide debt (think Enron and others).

It is best to leave corporate bonds to professional managers. You should think about purchasing either an open-end mutual fund or an exchange-traded corporate bond fund such as Goldman Sachs Corporate Bond Exchange Traded Fund (Symbol: LQD).

Another problem the bond investor needs to be aware of is the "call" feature, which allows the issuer to recall the bonds before maturity and pay the investor his principal, any interest due, and a slight premium. A bond is never called unless the issuer wants to retire them early, when interest rates go down. Bonds that have call features are frequently called when interest rates decline because it is cost-effective for the issuer to recall the bonds and reissue new ones at lower interest rates.

Rising interest rates are the enemy of interest-bearing securities, especially long-term bonds. As interest rates rise, investors would prefer to purchase interest-bearing securities with larger coupons, which are the annual interest payment that a bond pays. For example, if a U.S. Treasury, due February 2014, has a 5% coupon, the bond pays 5% in interest per year. If you bought the above-mentioned U.S. Treasury when interest rates were at 5% and interest rates remained at 5% until the bond matured, your investment would not fluctuate in price. However, if interest rates rose to 6%, your bond would decrease approximately 12% in value.

When interest rates rise, bonds on the secondary markets drop in value because new bonds carry a coupon of 6%. What would be more attractive, a bond paying 5% or one paying 6% when interest rates are paying 6%? That is why older bonds fall in value so they can be competitive with newly issued bonds. If interest rates drop, then bonds become more valuable. If you are holding a bond that pays 5% per year in interest and interest rates decline to 4%, you are still getting paid 5%. Your bond becomes more valuable and you could sell it.

In fact, most bond managers manage their portfolios with total return in mind. They want the coupon because that's very important, but they also want a capital gain, which is made when they sell the bond for a profit (a capital loss is when the manager sells at a loss).

It is my opinion that interest-bearing securities should be a part of every portfolio because they are one of the major asset classes. I do not believe that interest-bearing securities should be traded, unless interest rates are forecasted to rise largely or the credit quality of the interest-bearing security is in question.

I advocate that the investor hold his or her interest-bearing securities to maturity and not try to achieve a capital gain from them. As an asset class, interest-bearing securities are for your "safer" money, or money to give you income. You have other asset class choices for capital appreciation.

Rising interest rates and inflation are the enemies of interest-bearing securities. As I have discussed before, inflation destroys purchasing power. Imagine if, in 1958, you purchased a General Motors 2% Coupon Bond due in 30 years. By 1977, your bond would have been worth 75% less than what you paid for it, because interest rates in 1977 were averaging 7%.

Since it is impossible to accurately forecast the future, it is best not to purchase any individual interest-bearing security or fund past 6 years in maturity.

A simple technique called "laddering" is a useful method by which to manage your interest-bearing securities portfolio. Take the total amount of money you want to invest and divide it by the number of years of the farthest maturing interest-bearing security. For example, if you have a 6-year laddered portfolio, you would divide the money you have to invest in interest-bearing securities by six. Taking 100% and dividing by six gives you an allocation of 16.6% of invested monies per year. Simply invest 16.6% in year one, 16.6% in year two, and so on until year six. When the money you have invested has matured at the end of year one, take the money due at the end of year one and invest it in interest-bearing securities in year six. See the example as presented below in Figure 19.

Sally Jones has $200,000 to invest in interest-bearing securities, and she wants to build a laddered portfolio. She would perform the following.

Figure 19
Example of a Laddered Bond Portfolio

$200,000 divided by 6 = 33.33%

Year One	$33,333.33
Year Two	$33,333.33
Year Three	$33,333.33
Year Four	$33,333.33
Year Five	$33,333.33
Year Six	$33,333.33
Total	**$200,000**

If you used funds, you would be wise to use a highly regarded bond fund with a well-respected portfolio manager, and keep the duration of the fund to six years.

"Duration" is a concept that professionals take into account when planning bond investments. It considers the time to maturity and the size of the coupon and is an important investment management tool because it is a very good indicator of interest rate risk.

Regardless of whether you purchase investment-bearing securities in a fund, or individual securities, you need to be aware of fees and commissions. High fees and commissions will greatly reduce the amount of income and, hence, the total return on your interest-bearing securities.

It is also imperative that you pay the least amount you can when it comes to investing in interest-bearing securities. You need to always investigate and ask, "What is my yield to maturity (which is the interest rate you will receive after you pay any commissions and fees to purchase the bond or fund) after commissions and fees?"

If you purchase individual interest-bearing securities, there won't be any commissions due the broker upon sale of the bond, since you will be holding the bond to maturity. If you choose to purchase a bond fund, then I recommend that you choose a no-load, low expense fund, or better yet, an exchange traded fund — or, in the alternate, use Vanguard funds.

Yield to Maturity (YTM) is critical when purchasing individual interest-bearing securities or funds.

When purchasing these types of securities and funds, it is important to compare the individual security or funds' YTM with the current interest rate. Your broker or adviser will give you the YTM for any interest-bearing security or fund. Comparative figures can also be found at: **www.bloomberg.com** or in the C section of *The Wall Street Journal.*

Some insurance salesmen want to convince the investor that annuities and or whole life policies are investment vehicles — they are not. Annuities in any form, fixed or variable, have always been more profitable to the insurance company and the salesman selling them than they are to the person buying them.

Fixed annuities pay interest for a set period, while variable annuities use equity mutual funds. Most annuities are loaded with high fees and expenses and generate a lot of commissions.

In periods of low interest rates, annuity companies like to entice buyers of fixed annuities with a higher interest rate than is available in the open market. In most cases, this interest rate is a teaser to get the unsuspecting buyer to purchase an annuity. Most of the time, if interest rates drop, the annuity company informs the annuity buyer that his interest rate is also going to be lowered. If interest rates rise, then the annuity company has the buyer locked in at a set interest rate for a long period. Subsequently, the buyer is stuck with an annuity set at a lower interest rate than what he can get in the open market.

Annuities are a bad investment, and insurance policies are designed for insurance, not investments. For purposes of our simple investment plan, we will discuss other interest-bearing investments.

Interest-bearing investments consist of money market accounts, certificates of deposits, bank savings accounts, Treasury Bills, Treasury notes, Treasury bonds, preferred stocks, corporate bonds, tax-free bonds, savings bonds, U.S. agency bonds, and some other exotic instruments that Wall Street financial engineers have concocted.

All interest-bearing instruments obviously pay interest and, for the most part, mature on a certain date. Some interest-bearing securities, such as money markets and savings accounts, never mature, and some auction- preferred stocks keep rolling over into new interest-bearing securities.

Savings Accounts

Most of us are familiar with the passbook savings account. All banks and thrifts have them, and they are simple. You deposit money, and you are paid some amount of interest. At the time of this writing, savings accounts are paying around 1% per annum. Not much, but in the late 1970s, passbook savings accounts were paying as much as 9%.

In federally insured banks, passbook savings accounts are insured to $100,000 in case the bank collapses. There are some Thrift & Loans (that are not FDIC insured), which pay a slightly higher rate of interest. I don't advise my clients to put their money in uninsured institutions — it isn't worth the tiny extra amount of interest. This type of money should be considered your ultra-safe money in case you need it quickly.

Banks also sell Certificates of Deposit (CDs), and many banks have a wide variation of them. You will need to hold most CDs until maturity in order to receive the interest and not incur penalties, while some banks permit early withdrawal without penalty.

In general, the bank pays you a higher interest rate than what a passbook would pay, if you agree to leave your money on deposit for a certain length of time. When the CD matures, your deposit can be renewed at the prevailing rate. All CDs in federally insured institutions are guaranteed up to $100,000.

The same is true for passbook accounts. CDs and passbook savings were the favored investments of our grandparents who clearly remember the Great Depression and its aftermath; hence, their conservative natures.

Bankers' Acceptance

There are also banks that sell "Bankers' Acceptance," which is a vehicle the bank uses to finance the sale of goods for merchants. It is generally safe, but not insured, and pays a slightly higher rate of interest than either passbook accounts or CDs.

In the late 1970s and early 1980s, Bankers' Acceptance was paying as high as 15%; but then, during this period, interest rates in general were extremely high due to the increase in U.S. inflation which, in 1979, reached 13% and at one point, interest rates reached 21%. Nobody wanted to lock in interest rates for a long period back then because the purchasing power of your investment was quickly eroded.

Commercial Paper

Large, well-established corporations use commercial paper to finance some of their short-term borrowing needs. A company with good credit such as General Motors or General Electric can borrow directly from the securities markets instead of borrowing from a bank, saving them a great deal of money. You can also purchase commercial paper through a number of banks and brokerage firms. Investment-grade commercial paper is widely held; and all money market funds, except those that are tax-free, use commercial paper.

Commercial paper is not insured against default; so if you're interested in this vehicle, it's wise to spread your risk by buying different issues. Depending on the issuer, the minimum amount of commercial paper that can be purchased is $25,000, and some issuers will not sell commercial paper in amounts less than $100,000. By using this investment, you can build your own money market account and keep the higher interest for yourself. However, any investment in commercial paper should be purchased from reputable dealers and carry an investment grade rating with it.

When buying commercial paper, the YTM should be kept at 180 days or less, preferably 90 days. Major rating agencies such as Moody's and Standard and Poor's (S&P) rate commercial paper based upon the issuer's ability to pay back principal and the timely payment of interest.

Although defaults are rare in investment grade commercial paper, there have been instances where commercial paper was given an investment grade and the issuer defaulted. A case in point: In the middle 1980s, Integrated Resources was given an investment grade rating of A1-P1 (which is the highest rating) by S&P. However, Integrated eventually defaulted on all of their commercial paper.

Commercial paper is an unsecured I.O.U. given by the issuer. I recommend to my clients that they only purchase paper rated at A1-P1; otherwise, it's not worth the risk.

In 1987, Chrysler Corporation issued commercial paper rated A2-P2, a lower rating, and never defaulted on their commercial paper obligations during that period of time. Remember, just like a money market, commercial paper is simply a parking place for your funds.

Money Market Accounts

We take the money market for granted; however, the Reserve Fund started the first money market in 1973 which, at the time, was an innovation. Soon after, Merrill Lynch expanded the idea through their vast network of brokers, and it caught on like wildfire with the public. Today, the money market is a staple within all brokerage accounts and banks.

Money market funds purchase investment-grade commercial paper with maturities of less than 180 days and can provide the investor with 24/7 liquidity. Although not designed to be used as a checking account, many investors use these in that manner nonetheless.

Several institutions that offer money markets have restrictions on withdrawals or on how many checks the accountholder can write, but there are as many other institutions that have no restrictions at all.

A number of mutual funds, such as tax-free money market or high yielding money market accounts, offer variations of the basic money market account.

The higher yielding account is less safe because many of them include commercial paper and short-term bonds that have low bond ratings. With short-term bonds, if interest rates rise, this type of money market may lose value.

Normally, a money market will do everything to keep its value at par. In other words, if you put in $1 when you withdraw your money, you should receive $1 and any applicable interest. However, when a money market fund makes bad investments and a commercial paper issuer defaults, the fund loses money — and so do you.

Although rare, there have been several instances where money funds "broke the buck barrier," and the mutual fund parent had to step in. The last thing a mutual fund wants is for word to get around that one of their funds broke the buck.

Generally, this leads to a mass exodus that can spell trouble for the entire mutual fund family. The Federal Deposit Insurance Corporation does not insure money market accounts as banks do; however, another U.S. government agency — Securities Investor Protection Corporation (SIPC) — does insure brokerage accounts against failure.

Money market accounts are insured at brokerage firms for up to $100,000. However, some brokerage accounts provide additional insurance above the $100,000 limit. The truth is that in the event of a large brokerage failure, there would not be enough insurance to pay off investors, which is why you should very carefully investigate the financial stability of the brokerage firm and divide your accounts between several. Money market accounts are good parking places for your cash and short-term requirements, but they shouldn't be considered good, long-term investments.

U.S. Government Obligations

The United States issues various interest-bearing securities to finance their budget deficits and/or agency needs. The most well-known is the U.S. Treasury Bill, which are sold at a discount. For example, you purchase $100,000 in face value of a T-Bill but pay less than the face, or approximately $98,000. The difference between the $100,000 and $98,000 is your interest, which is paid up front. The bill then matures at full face value. Treasury Bills have maturities of 90- and 180-days.

Treasury Notes are sold in 2-, 5-, and 10-year maturities and are not sold at a discount. They pay interest semi-annually. Although discontinued now, Treasury Bonds have 30-year maturities and pay interest semiannually.

One advantage that Treasury Bills, Notes, and Bonds have in common is that the interest is free from state income taxes. This could be important in high tax states, such as California and New York, although you still have to pay federal tax. When compared to taxable corporate, interest-bearing securities; money markets; commercial paper; bank CD's; passbook accounts; and Bankers' Acceptance, Treasuries often are a better buy. You will need to compare the after-tax return rate.

Another form of Treasuries are U.S. Agency Bills, Notes, and Bonds. These interest-bearing securities are issued by agencies of the U.S. Government and are used to finance some of the programs of that particular agency. As an illustration: Farm Credit Bank loans money to farmers, and the Tennessee Valley Authority (another Federal agency) supplies electricity in the Southeast region of the U.S.

U.S. Treasuries are backed by the full faith and credit of the U.S. Government while Agency Bills, Notes, and Bonds are not. Because of the intense political pressure that would result, it is unlikely that an agency would default. However, they do not offer the "full faith and credit" of the U.S. Government, so while agencies pay interest in the same fashion as Treasuries, the rate they pay is slightly higher.

Another form of U.S. Government debt is the savings bond, of which there are two types: Series EE and Series I. Both have a maturity of 30 years and pay interest when cashed in. An advantage of savings bonds is that the tax on the interest can be deferred until the bond is cashed in and, like Treasuries and agencies, it is free from state income tax. Currently, Series EE Bonds pay interest at the rate equal to 85% of the five-year U.S. Treasury notes.

I-Bonds offer built-in inflation protection. The I-Bond pays a base rate every six months, and adjusts that rate based on the Consumer Price Index. You can purchase either the Series EE or I-Bond in denominations of $25 or more, for a total of $33,000 of each. A couple could purchase a total of $66,000 in I-Bonds and $66,000 in Series EE each year.

Treasury Inflation Protected Securities (TIPS) are the first cousin to I-Bonds and come in denominations of $5,000 and more; there is no limit on how much you can purchase. TIPS work in the same fashion as I-Bonds except the maturities of TIPS is 10 years.

If you believe that inflation will occur in the future, I-Bonds and TIPS become good choices because they will help protect your purchasing power. However, there are times to purchase, and times not to purchase, I-Bonds and TIPS. For example, when the base rate of interest paid is low, TIPS and I-Bonds should be avoided. Case in point: In January 2004, the base rate for TIPS was 1.5%. Add the inflation rate of 1%, and your total return is 2.5%, a figure too low since inflation over the long run averages approximately 4%.

If you were interested in TIPS, you would want to wait until the base rate was between 2.5% and 3% or more before purchasing them. The same holds true for I-Bonds.

You can purchase TIPS or I-Bonds directly from the U.S. Government at their Web site, **www.treasurydirect.gov,** saving you the brokerage and transaction costs! You can even pay with your credit card and earn miles.

I believe that I-Bonds and TIPS should be part of every portfolio because they can help you retain your purchasing power.

Tax Free Interest-Bearing Issues

Cities, counties, states, and other municipalities fund their public works and civic projects with tax-bonds, which they can do at a lower cost to them because the interest earned by the investor is generally tax-free, both federally and by the state.

In New York City, if you purchase a State of New York tax-free bond, it is free from city, state, and federal taxes (known as "triple tax-free"). If you live in California and purchase an Arizona tax-free bond, you would be required to pay California state income tax on the interest received. To be completely state and federal tax-free, you need to purchase tax-free issues in the state in which you reside.

There are three types of tax-free issues: General Obligation, Revenue, and Industrial Development Bonds. General Obligation Bonds are supposedly the safest because the issuer has the authority to increase taxes to pay both the interest and principal of the bond. However, as we have seen in Orange County, California, when the County defaulted on their obligations, General Obligation Bonds were not immune from risk. However, in this particular case, the bonds eventually were paid off with extra interest to compensate holders. The risk in most General Obligation Bonds, in strong governmental agencies, is nominal.

Revenue Bonds are dependent upon the revenue generated by the project the bond was intended to pay so, by nature, these are more risky than General Obligation Bonds. For example, California issued Golden Gate Revenue Bonds to make some additions to, and repair the Golden Gate Bridge in San Francisco. Each toll collected to cross the bridge goes to help pay the interest and principal of the Golden Gate Bridge District Revenue Bond. However, if an earthquake destroys the Golden Gate Bridge, there would be no revenue to pay off the bond, and the issue could go into default.

The most risky of all tax-free bonds are Industrial Development and Special District Bonds. To attract industry to their communities, municipalities sell industrial Development Bonds. Case in point: The City of Irvine, California, let Mazda Motor Company finance part of their design facilities within the city by letting them sell tax-free bonds, bringing some desirable business to Irvine and giving Mazda a big tax break by subsidizing a portion of the applicable interest.

If Mazda had encountered any problems whereby they could not have paid back the interest or principal, they, and not the City, would still have been responsible for payments.

Another form of Development Bonds are those that land developers use to raise money to build the infrastructure in new neighborhoods. Before the 1980s, most developers who built neighborhoods from the ground up paid for the roads, parks, and schools, and built the cost of their infrastructure into the selling price of the home. Not any more. Developers sell bonds to pay for the infrastructure they build. Because these bonds can be very risky, I advise my clients not to bother with special district or industrial development bonds. The little amount of extra interest you will receive isn't worth the extra risk.

Corporate Bonds are issued by companies seeking to finance their operations through debt; they are rated according to the corporation's ability to pay back the principal and interest on a timely basis. The two main rating agencies are Standard and Poor's (S&P) and Moody's, the latter of which rates investment grade bonds with the letters AAA through BBB, while S&P simply uses A through B. Obviously, A is a higher grade than B, and anything below B is considered a high-yield bond, which are commonly referred to as "junk bonds."

Bonds that are graded B and below are considered junk because of the company's relative inability to pay interest and principal. This particular field of investment is strictly for professionals and is not suited for individuals looking for a simplified investment plan.

If an investor were to invest in junk bonds, they should be made through mutual funds and with a diversification in junk, through two or more funds. The junk bond portfolio manager should have an outstanding reputation and many years of experience. The fees for entry into a well-managed fund will be more than if the investor purchased a poorly managed fund. Obviously, you are paying for the manager's ability to navigate through a world of distressed securities. It is well worth the extra cost!

Many investors make the same mistake and buy junk bond funds at the wrong time. These investors purchase junk bond funds when interest rates start to decline, hoping to "lock in" a higher rate of interest. Yet, this is exactly the wrong time to purchase junk funds. Rather, the time to buy them is when the economy has bottomed out and is turning around.

The quality of junk bonds improves with the economy because various companies' abilities to pay back principal and interest are improved when a company's prospects are getting better. Generally, an improved economy will benefit a company that is in financial trouble, more than one that is already doing well. Companies that are not in financial trouble do not have a problem raising debt capital — nor do they need to pay the higher interest rates that junk bonds command.

Interest-bearing securities are an important asset class for each investor. The premise of this book is to provide a simple investment plan suitable for most investors.

Although there are a variety of investment choices in interest-bearing securities, it would undoubtedly be best for you to put your money in the obligations of the United States Government, a number of selected tax-free issues (especially in New York and California), and in TIPS — and your portfolio should be laddered and have maturities no longer than 6 years.

13

Indexing
The simplest
way to invest

The debate rages on, and probably always will: Is a passive investing approach using indexing better for most investors, or is a more aggressive approach in which the investor picks and chooses individual stocks, a superior plan?

In my opinion, for most individuals and investment managers, indexing or passive management is best. I spend most of my working day, some nights and weekends too, hunting for good investments. It is very time consuming. If you don't want to work as hard as I do, then the simplest and safer route is to index your equity, real estate and commodity investments. If a manager can add value by picking individual stocks, then active management is preferable. However, as we have seen, most professionals can't add value — so what makes you so sure you can?

Passive management reduces expenses, but even passive management has its pitfalls. For example, an investor may choose the passive investment style and choose several or more index funds. However, without some degree of knowledge and expertise, the investor may not diversify his portfolio properly or, worse, get in several index funds and index sectors at the wrong time.

Active investment management is when portfolio managers search for what they believe to be promising stocks. A number of mutual funds and advisers prefer growth stocks, while others like to choose value equities. They may restrict their selections to large capitalization or possibly small capitalization, or something in between. Regardless of their style, advisers who practice active management are attempting to beat the market.

Passive investment management does not even bother to try to beat the market. Indexers (as some passive investment managers are called) just want to equal whatever benchmark they are emulating.

Although it is possible for an active manager to beat the market (and a good number of portfolio managers do), there are significantly more who do not beat their respective benchmark.

Several academic studies have concluded that the majority of investment and mutual fund managers cannot consistently beat the market.

Professor Michael C. Jensen authored a paper titled *The Performance of Mutual Funds*, which examined the performance of equity mutual funds between 1945 and 1964. He concluded that 80% of all equity funds could not outperform the S&P 500 index during that time.

In another study conducted by SEI Corporation during the period between 1970 and 1992, equity mutual funds returned 10.8% while the total stock market, as represented by the Wilshire 5000, returned 12%.

Many additional studies by academics and practicing managers show similar results. After examining the Jensen and SEI studies, it is clear that the majority of money managers cannot outperform their benchmarks because of transaction costs and many managers' lack of talent.

Beware: Funds with aggressive, stock-picking managers charge more than index funds. There are funds, however, whose managers hew too closely to benchmark indexes. Investors in these funds are then stuck with both the higher cost of a true aggressive fund and the lower returns of a true index fund. These are referred to as "closet indexers."

Beating the Market

While there are always those managers who consistently beat the market, it is a rare occurrence, and identifying those individuals is difficult. There are several reasons why even a fund that has consistently beat the market eventually falls to mediocrity. One reason is size. When a fund is small, it has the opportunity to locate and discover stocks not on most managers' radar screens. The small fund can buy less liquid stocks because they do not have as much money to invest and, thus, can move in and out of positions rapidly, with much more liquidity, than the larger funds.

As a fund grows in popularity, the fund has to buy larger capitalization stocks so that the manager can purchase meaningful positions. For example, could the manager of Fidelity's Magellan Fund purchase shares of Consolidated Tomoka, a company that trades maybe 1,000 shares per day, and buy a meaningful number of shares that would affect Magellan's performance? The answer is no. The manager of Magellan would have to buy large cap stocks — like Ford, Microsoft, or Home Depot — that are picked over and examined by the multitudes of other managers and investors.

According to Lipper Analytical Services and The Institute for Business and Finance, the majority of actively managed funds fail to beat the market, and only 31% of all general equity funds beat the S&P 500. In 10 years, from 1990 to 2000, the number of actively managed funds that beat the S&P fell to 18%. This is a dismal record, and it leads me to believe that for most investors, indexing is a preferred asset class for bonds, stocks, and commodities.

The "Efficient Market Hypothesis" Controversy

The underperformance of many of the mutual funds, especially the larger funds and those that are classified as large capitalization, is due to the "Efficient Market Hypothesis" (EMH). In simplest terms, The Efficient Market Hypothesis states that all of the information about a security is reflected in the price of that security and that since any information about that security is reflected in the pricing mechanism, it is all but impossible to obtain an above-average return.

The EMH is extremely controversial within academic circles and with practitioners. Many believe the EMH is true and, therefore, it is futile for investors to actively manage portfolios by individually selecting stocks. Put simply, they should just index their portfolios.

Benjamin Graham, who has been called the twentieth century's most outstanding investor, wrote in *The Intelligent Investor* that he is now a proponent of the EMH. This is quite a statement, coming from a man who spent his whole career beating the market by a wide margin.

Others, like John Bogle of Vanguard, also believe that the EMH is true and that active managers cannot beat the market. Still others, like Warren Buffett, believe the EMH theory is garbage. Buffett stated in his article *The Super Investors of Graham and Doddsville,* which is published as an appendix to *The Intelligent Investor,* that he believes the EMH is a bunch of rubbish conjured up by a bunch of professors in ivory towers.

I believe as others do, that there are some who can consistently beat the market. I have consistently beaten the market, albeit not every single year, but in the long-term. However, in doing so, I expend an extraordinary amount of time and effort reading about, and researching my securities. The proponents of the EMH believe that active management is not worth the time and expense. The truth lies somewhere in the middle.

Those managers who beat the index, limit the amount of money they manage and, thus, they usually troll for stocks in areas that are inefficiently priced. For the most part, those inefficient areas of the stock market are Large, Mid and Small Capitalization Value stocks and foreign securities.

It doesn't matter if you believe that the market is efficient or not, or that an active manager can beat the market. I believe that for "most" investors, indexing is a preferred method versus active management. I believe this because simplicity is at the heart of my financial philosophy, and an indexed portfolio is about as simple as investing gets.

Accounting Shenanigans Are Still Alive

Even if the investor believes that the market is inefficient, it is time-consuming and difficult to analyze individual securities. Today, securities and companies have become too complex for the average, untrained investor to analyze and comprehend.

It is even becoming complex for professionals. According to Business Week, in their October 4, 2004 edition, they stated that today's financial reports are more difficult than ever to understand.

Donna Vickery, a former accounting professor and co-founder of Research Alliance Inc., a Scottsdale, Arizona, firm hired by institutional investors, said in the Business Week article: "Reports are riddled with jargon that's hard to fathom and numbers that don't track. They're muddled, with inconsistent categories, vague entries, and hidden adjustments that disguise how much various estimates change a company's earnings from quarter to quarter.

"There have been several times in which it was difficult for me to interpret the information in the annual reports and 10-K (a company's government filing to the SEC). For example, in 1999 I was researching Enron because some of my portfolio manager friends had Enron, and they told me I was crazy not to have it in my portfolio. Instead of listening to them, I wanted to research it myself. I could not figure it out, but I knew something was amiss, although I could not pinpoint exactly what, so I skipped buying Enron and, boy, am I glad I did.

"The point being, I was not able to figure out what was going on in Enron so I never bought it, but there were many professionals and non-professionals alike who did buy Enron, and they got burned."

Not all is lost, though, because the use of exchange-traded funds and other mutual funds provides a great solution to those who do not have the time, inclination, or ability to analyze individual securities.

For my personal investment funds, as well as those of my clients, I prefer to be an active investment manager; but I have good reason for this. For one, I have demonstrated over long periods that I can outperform equity benchmarks. However, to do so, I spend an inordinate amount of time reading and analyzing securities and the economic trends of the world markets. In order for me to beat the markets, I spend on average of 10 hours or more every day analyzing equities. Most people don't have the drive or interest to put that much effort and work into selecting stocks. I, on the other hand, do it because I love it!

For our simplified investment plan, the use of exchange-traded funds and individual bonds will provide a very good, if not unexciting, investment platform, suitable for most investors.

14

Mutual Funds and Exchange Traded Funds

There are three basic fund types: Exchange traded funds (ETF), open-end, and closed-end mutual funds, each of which has its own characteristics, expense ratios, and suitability. For investors not using active management, my first preference is to use Exchange traded funds, followed by closed-end funds, and then open-end mutual funds.

"If abnormal returns are promised, there must be abnormal risk."

–Hobart Rowan

Exchange Traded Funds

Exchange traded funds (ETF), especially index funds, use passive investment management. Their function is to emulate an index and to keep their expenses low, something open-end mutual funds rarely do. Actually, Exchange traded funds are a combination of an open-end fund and a closed-end fund, the result being the combined best of both.

Exchange traded funds trade during market hours on exchanges similar to individual stocks and closed-end funds. However, ETF expenses are low and like open-end mutual funds, shares on the open market can be sold in any quantity. Except in a limited number of cases, there is no reason to use open-end mutual funds when the investor can purchase and sell Exchange traded funds. Not only will the cost be lower but Exchange traded funds are more liquid since the investor can buy and sell them during market hours instead of having to wait until the market closes to buy and sell.

Some Exchange traded funds have monikers like Spiders, Diamonds, and Qubes; but essentially, all Exchange traded funds trade on exchanges — and since they trade like stocks, they can be bought and sold (always through a broker) like stocks throughout the day.

One of the best features of Exchange traded funds is that for the most part, their expense ratios are low, much lower than no-load funds. The exception to this is that some specialty exchange traded closed-end funds have high expense ratios. Therefore, it is imperative that the investor determine if he is buying an Exchange traded fund or a closed-end fund that is disguised as an Exchange traded fund.

The American Stock Exchange is home to many of the most popular Exchange traded funds (see Figure 20 for a sample list). Because the popularity of Exchange traded funds is growing, the New York Stock Exchange lists them as well. Other global exchanges such as Toronto and London have their version of Exchange traded funds. The American Stock Exchange Web site is **www.amex.com**; the New York Stock Exchange, **www.NYSE.com**.

Exchange traded funds are becoming popular because they are liquid, trade easily, and have low expense ratios. Any investor can assemble a diversified portfolio using Exchange traded funds.

An alternative to Exchange traded funds are index funds. The leader in index funds with low expense charges is Vanguard. For example, some asset sub-sectors don't have Exchange traded funds, so the investor would have to choose no load funds. Vanguard is the preferred choice because of their integrity and low expense ratios.

Figure 20

Exchange Traded Funds on the American Stock Exchange

Product Name	Symbol	Category	Issuer
DIAMONDS	DIA	Broad based	PDR Services LLC

Product Name	Symbol	Category	Issuer
FORTUNE 500 Index Tracking Stock	FFF	Broad based	State Street
Mid-Cap SPDRS	MDY	Broad based	PDR Services LLC
Nasdaq-100 Index Tracking Stock	QQQ	Broad based	NASDAQ Financial Products Services, Inc
PowerShares Dynamic Market Portfolio	PWC	Broad based	PowerShares Exchange-Trade Fund Trust
PowerShares Dynamic OTC Portfolio	PWO	Broad based	PowerShares Exchange-Trade Fund Trust
Rydex S&P Equal Weight ETF	RSP	Broad based	Rydex ETF Trust
SPDRS	SPY	Broad based	PDR Services LLC
Select Sector SPDR-Consumer Discretionary	XLY	Sector	State Street
Select Sector SPDR-Consumer Staples	XLP	Sector	State Street
Select Sector SPDR-Energy	XLE	Sector	State Street
Select Sector SPDR-Financial	XLF	Sector	State Street
Select Sector SPDR-Health Care	XLV	Sector	State Street
Select Sector SPDR-Industrial	XLI	Sector	State Street
Select Sector SPDR-Materials	XLB	Sector	State Street
Select Sector SPDR-Technology	XLK	Sector	State Street
Select Sector SPDR-Utilities	XLU	Sector	State Street

Product Name	Symbol	Category	Issuer
Vanguard Consumer Discretionary VIPERs	VCR	Sector	Vanguard
Vanguard Consumer Staples VIPERs	VDC	Sector	Vanguard
Vanguard Extended Market VIPERs	VXF	Broad based	Vanguard
Vanguard Financials VIPERs	VFH	Sector	Vanguard
Vanguard Growth VIPERs	VUG	Broad based	Vanguard
Vanguard Health Care VIPERs	VHT	Sector	Vanguard
Vanguard Information Technology VIPERs	VGT	Sector	Vanguard
Vanguard Large-Cap VIPERs	VV	Broad based	Vanguard
Vanguard Materials VIPERs	VAW	Sector	Vanguard
Vanguard Mid-Cap VIPERs	VO	Broad based	Vanguard
Vanguard Small-Cap Growth VIPERs	VBK	Broad based	Vanguard
Vanguard Small-Cap VIPERs	VB	Broad based	Vanguard
Vanguard Small-Cap Value VIPERs	VBR	Broad based	Vanguard
Vanguard Total Stock Market VIPERs	VTI	Broad based	Vanguard
Vanguard Utilities VIPERs	VPU	Sector	Vanguard

Product Name	Symbol	Category	Issuer
Vanguard Value VIPERs	VTV	Broad based	Vanguard
iShares Cohen & Steers Realty Majors	ICF	Sector	BGI
iShares Dow Jones Transportation Average Index Fund	IYT	Sector	iShares Trust
iShares Dow Jones US Basic Materials	IYM	Sector	BGI
iShares Dow Jones US Consumer Cyclical	IYC	Sector	BGI
iShares Dow Jones US Consumer Non-Cyclical	IYK	Sector	BGI
iShares Dow Jones US Energy	IYE	Sector	BGI
iShares Dow Jones US Financial Sector	IYF	Sector	BGI
iShares Dow Jones US Financial Services	IYG	Sector	BGI
iShares Dow Jones US Healthcare	IYH	Sector	BGI
iShares Dow Jones US Industrial	IYJ	Sector	BGI
iShares Dow Jones US Real Estate	IYR	Sector	BGI
iShares Dow Jones US Technology	IYW	Sector	BGI
iShares Dow Jones US Telecommunications	IYZ	Sector	BGI
iShares Dow Jones US Total Market	IYY	Broad based	BGI

Product Name	Symbol	Category	Issuer
iShares Dow Jones US Utilities	IDU	Sector	BGI
iShares GS $ InvesTop™ Corporate Bond Fund	LQD	Broad based	BGI
iShares Goldman Sachs Natural Resources	IGE	Sector	BGI
iShares Goldman Sachs Networking	IGN	Sector	BGI
iShares Goldman Sachs Semiconductor	IGW	Sector	BGI
iShares Goldman Sachs Software	IGV	Sector	BGI
iShares Goldman Sachs Technology	IGM	Sector	BGI
iShares Lehman 1-3 Year Treasury Bond Fund	SHY	Broad based	BGI
iShares Lehman 20+ Year Treasury Bond Fund	TLT	Broad based	BGI
iShares Lehman 7-10 Year Treasury Bond Fund	IEF	Broad based	BGI
iShares Lehman Aggregate Bond Fund	AGG	Broad based	iShares Trust
iShares MSCI Emerging Markets	EEM	International	BGI

Product Name	Symbol	Category	Issuer
iShares MSCI-Australia	EWA	International	BGI
iShares MSCI-Austria	EWO	International	BGI
iShares MSCI-Belgium	EWK	International	BGI
iShares MSCI-Brazil	EWZ	International	BGI
iShares MSCI-Canada	EWC	International	BGI
iShares MSCI-EAFE	EFA	International	BGI
iShares MSCI-EMU	EZU	International	BGI
iShares MSCI-France	EWQ	International	BGI
iShares MSCI-Germany	EWG	International	BGI
iShares MSCI-Hong Kong	EWH	International	BGI
iShares MSCI-Italy	EWI	International	BGI
iShares MSCI-Japan	EWJ	International	BGI
iShares MSCI-Malaysia	EWM	International	BGI
iShares MSCI-Mexico	EWW	International	BGI
iShares MSCI-Netherlands	EWN	International	BGI
iShares MSCI-Pacific Ex-Japan	EPP	International	BGI
iShares MSCI-Singapore	EWS	International	BGI
iShares MSCI-South Africa	EZA	International	BGI
iShares MSCI-South Korea	EWY	International	BGI
iShares MSCI-Spain	EWP	International	BGI
iShares MSCI-Sweden	EWD	International	BGI

Product Name	Symbol	Category	Issuer
iShares MSCI-Switzerland	EWL	International	BGI
iShares MSCI-Taiwan	EWT	International	BGI
iShares MSCI-U.K.	EWU	International	BGI
iShares Nasdaq Biotechnology	IBB	Sector	BGI
iShares Russell 1000	IWB	Broad based	BGI
iShares Russell 1000 Growth	IWF	Broad based	BGI
iShares Russell 1000 Value	IWD	Broad based	BGI
iShares Russell 2000	IWM	Broad based	BGI
iShares Russell 2000 Growth	IWO	Broad based	BGI
iShares Russell 2000 Value	IWN	Broad based	BGI
iShares Russell 3000	IWV	Broad based	BGI
iShares Russell 3000 Growth	IWZ	Broad based	BGI
iShares Russell 3000 Value	IWW	Broad based	BGI
iShares Russell Mid-cap Growth Index Fund	IWP	Broad based	BGI
iShares Russell Mid-cap Index Fund	IWR	Broad based	BGI
iShares Russell Mid-cap Value Index Fund	IWS	Broad based	BGI
iShares S&P 100 Index Fund	OEF	Broad based	BGI

Product Name	Symbol	Category	Issuer
iShares S&P 1500 Index Fund	ISI	Broad based	N.A.
iShares S&P 500	IVV	Broad based	BGI
iShares S&P 500 BARRA Growth	IVW	Broad based	BGI
iShares S&P 500 BARRA Value	IVE	Broad based	BGI
iShares S&P Europe 350	IEV	International	BGI
iShares S&P Global Energy Sector	IXC	Sector	BGI
iShares S&P Global	IXG	Sector	BGIFinancial Sector
iShares S&P Global Healthcare Sector	IXJ	Sector	BGI
iShares S&P Global Information Technology Sector	IXN	Sector	BGI
iShares S&P Global Telecommunications Sector	IXP	Sector	BGI
iShares S&P Latin America 40	ILF	International	BGI
iShares S&P Madcap 400	IJH	Broad based	BGI
iShares S&P Madcap 400/BARRA Growth	IJK	Broad based	BGI
iShares S&P Madcap 400/BARRA Value	IJJ	Broad based	BGI
iShares S&P Small Cap 600	IJR	Broad based	BGI

Product Name	Symbol	Category	Issuer
iShares S&P Small Cap 600 BARRA Growth	IJT	Broad based	BGI
iShares S&P Small Cap 600 BARRA Value	IJS	Broad based	BGI
iShares S&P/ TOPIX 150	ITF	International	BGI
streetTRACKS Dow Jones Global Titans 50 Index	DGT	Broad based	State Street
streetTRACKS Dow Jones US LargeCap Growth	ELG	Broad based	State Street
streetTRACKS Dow Jones US LargeCap Value	ELV	Broad based	State Street
streetTRACKS Dow Jones US SmallCap Growth	DSG	Broad based	State Street
streetTRACKS Dow Jones US SmallCap Value	DSV	Broad based	State Street
streetTRACKS Morgan Stanley Technology	MTK	Sector	State Street
streetTRACKS Wilshire REIT	RWR	Sector	State Street

Source: American Stock Exchange Web site: **www.amex.com**

Closed-end Funds

Closed-end funds are like stocks. The investment company that sponsors the closed-end fund sells a limited number of shares, and the shares trade on an Exchange. Unless a company issues additional shares through a rights offering, the number of closed-end shares are set and will not be increased.

The investors in closed-end shares have the same liquidity as individuals using securities or Exchange traded funds. The investment adviser for the fund charges the fund directly for his management fee. The investor needs to be aware that a number of closed-end funds charge high management fees, and their expense ratios can be larger than some of their open-end mutual fund cousins. However, while all open-end mutual funds bought and sold are at net asset value (the value of all securities and cash in the fund during any trading day), closed-end funds can sell at a premium or discount to net asset value. Closed-end funds trade at various times at a premium or discount, depending on market sentiment.

The intelligent investor shouldn't buy a closed-end fund at a premium but should wait until the discount is 10% or more. Essentially, buying closed-end funds at a discount is a great way to buy the same thing as an open-end mutual fund, but cheaper. For example, let's say that an investor wants to buy the Tri-Continental Closed-end Fund (TRI). This fund is the same as any growth fund with the one difference being that you can buy Tri-Continental at an 18% discount to the value of the fund's holdings. In other words, the investor gets to buy $1 worth of assets for 82 cents. You can find a complete listing of closed end mutual funds in Barron's weekly.

When purchasing open-end funds, the investor needs to be very careful when making his selection. Since the investor is paying for active management, he wants to be assured that he is getting good performance for what he's paying. (See the section earlier in this book entitled "Closet Indexer.")

When I select mutual funds, I compare several statistics among the funds in which I am interested. These statistics, as listed below, aid me greatly during the selection process.

Morningstar Rating (1-5)

Morningstar was the first company to rate mutual funds based upon performance and risk. Their information has proven to be so reliable, it is now an industry standard and as such, many professionals use Morningstar information to help them in their selection process.

Morningstar rates funds, using a star system, based on risk-adjusted returns for 3 and 5 years. A 5-star fund is the best rating. A 1-star, the lowest a fund can have.

Using the Morningstar rating system, in conjunction with some of the other measures I have discussed, can be very helpful. However, to use the Morningstar ratings alone would be a mistake. Since over 45% of all funds that had superior performance one year went on to mediocre performance the next. Selecting funds on Morningstar ratings alone would not be a wise approach. As an illustration: Many gold funds in recent years have received a 2-star Morningstar rating because gold had a poor performance record for almost 20 years. However, during the past three years, gold has been one of the better performing asset classes.

However, if a Morningstar rating is 1- or 2-stars and the fund is a specialty fund correlated to the stock market, it probably should be avoided. In addition, many 3-star funds are mediocre performers.

When I discuss the Jensen index (Alpha) shortly, it will become apparent that unless a 3-star fund produces positive Alpha, it should be avoided.

Risk Measures

A nominal rate of return by itself doesn't mean much. What counts is how much risk a portfolio manager took to get the return. Therefore, any mutual fund investor needs to consider the degree of risk that was taken for a given performance and make adjustments.

For example, one investor achieved a 14% rate of return while another received a 9% rate of return. Which return is better? Most of you would take the 14% versus the 9% rate of return. However, the truth lies in the investment itself. The 14% rate of return was in a gold mine, while the 9% was in stocks. The gold mine was definitely more risky, and it did not warrant an investment. A real measure of a portfolio manager's ability is his capacity or talent to invest with *minimized* risk.

There are several useful techniques for analyzing risk and return: Sharpe Ratio, Standard Deviation, Beta, and Jensen (Alpha) Index.

William Sharpe, a Stanford professor of finance, was the first to recognize the effects of risk in investing. He developed the Sharpe Ratio to relate the return of an investment, or portfolio, to the degree of total risk.

The higher the quotient, the greater return for each unit. The Sharpe Ratio should be positive. For anyone interested in the specific formula, any college level investment textbook will have it; however, the formula itself is not what's important here. The Sharpe Ratio by itself is of little use to the investor. However, used in comparison with other investments or mutual funds, it becomes significant. When the return on the market is used in the formula, a mutual fund can be compared to a market return. For example, a mutual fund manager that had a higher quotient than the market would have beaten the market on a risk-adjusted basis.

The Jensen Ratio compares the expected return with the actual return — the difference of which is called the "Alpha." The Alpha indicates the additional return earned by an investment or mutual fund after adjusting for risk.

A high Alpha — especially a positive one — is considered good and means that the portfolio produced a greater return than its risk. A positive Alpha indicates the portfolio manager outperformed the market on a risk-adjusted basis. Sometimes Alphas are negative, which doesn't mean the portfolio manager had a negative performance but, rather, that the portfolio performance was less than expected, given the amount of risk the portfolio manager took.

Beta is a measure of risk or price volatility. The higher the Beta, the more volatile a portfolio or security will be; and, conversely, the lower the Beta, the lower the volatility.

Beta is a controversial measurement that is sometimes not a reliable indicator, especially within a short timeframe. However, it is a good approximation of price volatility in a security, port-folio, or fund.

In certain cases, price volatility can be your friend because it enables you to purchase shares at a lower price. For example, Salomon Brothers was a very volatile stock and had a high Beta. The price moved up and down in volatile spurts from 28 on the low side to 50 on the high side, in a short period.

If an investor wanted to increase his position in Salomon, he could either wait until the price reached 38 or so, or buy some shares at a higher price and then buy more as the price declined.

In this case, price volatility worked in the investor's favor. Stocks that have a Beta over 1 are more volatile than stocks that have a beta of .80. As an illustration, Green Mountain Power has a Beta of .80, which means that when the market as measured by the S&P 500 moves up, Green Mountain Power moves up 20% less than the market. When the market moves down, Green Mountain moves down 20% less than the market. What is important to remember here is that Beta can be used to meas-ure the price volatility of your mutual fund.

Standard Deviation (SD) is a statistical measurement to deter-mine price volatility.

By itself, Standard Deviation means little to the investor; but when compared to another benchmark, it becomes a useful tool to determine risk. For example, if a fund has a standard devia-tion of 15.3 and the stock market has a standard deviation of 19.6, the fund has a lower risk profile. So this is how we can use SD to our advantage when comparing funds to their benchmark and when comparing funds and individual securities between themselves.

All funds and their portfolio managers are compared to a benchmark which is simply some index that is close to the type of fund the portfolio manages. For example, Fidelity Magellan Fund's benchmark is the S&P 500, while Longleaf Partners Fund benchmark is the S&P Mid-cap 400.

Although the S&P 500 and the Dow Jones Industrial Average are the most widely quoted and used benchmarks, they are not appropriate for every fund. Case in point: A small capitalization fund using the S&P 500 benchmark would be inappropriate because the S&P is comprised of large capitalization companies. A small capitalization fund, on the other hand, might use a benchmark such as the Russell 2000.

Services such as Morningstar use what is called a "best fit benchmark," which is the performance index most closely aligned to the type of fund to which it is being compared. It is best to use a best fit benchmark when evaluating a fund's performance.

R-squared measures a fund's proximity to its benchmark. In other words, are the fund's performance and holdings close to its closest fit benchmark, or does the portfolio attempt to provide the best value for the shareholder by thinking independently? Does the portfolio manager want to maximize the fund's returns by concentrating his positions and/or buying what he thinks will be a good security, or does he try to emulate a benchmark so he does not fall too far behind his peers? The closer the squared figure (use Morningstar to find the R-square) is to its "best fit" benchmark number, the more the fund becomes like an index fund. You don't want to pay management fees for closet indexers. Choose funds that have R-squared numbers that are not close to their benchmark.

Like individual investors, portfolio managers tend to think and move in herds. If a manager falls too far behind a benchmark for a long period, the fund may lose many of its assets, and the portfolio manager will either be fired or certainly not get his bonus.

Therefore, many portfolio managers want their performance to follow their benchmark. In order to do so, they will construct their portfolio to emulate the index, but may tweak it in an attempt to outperform the benchmark by a small margin.

If the portfolio manager can match the index (a difficult thing to do), then he will beat 85% of his peers. If the portfolio manager constructs his portfolio differently than his index and his securities don't perform well, then he will fall behind (and be in trouble!), which is why so many portfolio managers emulate their indexes.

Let's take a real life example from Morningstar — Longleaf Partners Fund (LLPFX) — and see how we can learn from some of these exotic-sounding risk measures: Looking at the data in Figure 21 below, Longleaf has an R-squared number of 68, which is far enough from the best index number of 76. LLPFX is not a closet index fund. The Beta is lower than the Beta of the S&P 500. The Alpha for Longleaf is a whopping 9.05, which shows that the manager has delivered value. The Sharpe Ratio is positive, so its risk-adjusted return is also positive. The Standard Deviation of 15.22 for LLPFX is lower than the Standard Deviation of the market, which is 20.

Even though Morningstar rates Longleaf Partners Fund 3-stars, this manager adds real value and does not follow the herd. He earns his fee. (By the way, Longleaf Partners fund is a value fund.)

Figure 21
Risk Measures for Longleaf Partners Fund

	LLPFX vs S&P 500	LLPFX vs S&P 400
Mid-capitalization Index		
R-squared	68	76
Beta	.75	.79
Alpha	9.05	3.04
Standard Deviation	15.52	15.55
Sharpe Ratio	.72	n/a

Duration measures the price sensitivity of a bond or bond fund to a change in interest rates. The shorter the duration, the less risky a bond portfolio becomes. Longer-term bonds are more sensitive to interest rates. For example, if a bond portfolio has a duration of 15 and interest rates rise 1%, then the portfolio will most likely lose 15%. Using the same duration of 15%, if interest rates rise 2%, then the bond portfolio will lose a whopping 30%.

Imagine bond investors having a duration of 15 in their bond portfolio and interest rates rise 3%. In this case, their portfolios could decline 45%. It is best to keep bond fund and bond durations below 6.

Subtitle Fees

Over time, excessive fees erode the performance return of the portfolio. Fees paid by the investor to the mutual fund are the biggest single item overlooked by the mutual fund investor. Many mutual funds charge marketing fees (called 12b-1 fees) that compensate brokers to put clients in no load funds.

Excessive fees reduce portfolio performance, especially over long periods when compounding takes effect. Many funds and their advisors abuse the 12b-1-fee ruling and charge excessive and unwarranted 12b-1 fees. Choose funds that have low expenses.

Excessive fees, in my opinion, are a detriment to portfolio performance. For domestic large capitalization equity funds, total expense ratios should not be over 1%. For small capitalization equity funds, the total expense ratio should be less than 1.25%. Foreign equity funds should not have an expense ratio over 1.75%. Specialty funds like precious metals have a higher expense ratio, sometimes approaching 2%.

This is why I prefer Exchange traded funds because the expense ratios are very low. Why buy a fund when the expense ratio is high when you can get the same performance on an index fund from Vanguard or an Exchange traded fund with low expenses?

Vanguard Mutual Funds is a company actually owned by the shareholders. It is a mutual company and because of its status, the expense ratios of its funds are the lowest of any fund family. If you must invest in no load mutual funds, then I suggest you use Vanguard.

There are two types of open-end mutual funds. One is load, the other is no load. Load funds charge the investors commissions, which are then paid to the salesmen who sell them. Commissions are not charged on no load funds. Most of the time, the investor can buy an excellent no load fund that has the same performance as a load fund.

There have been a considerable number of academic studies done that compare the performance of load and no load funds. In each study, there was no evidence that load funds outperformed no load funds. Unless he wants to support his broker, there is rarely a reason for an investor to purchase a load fund.

Load funds come in different classes such as A through F. During the past few years, a large number of brokers were abusing their customers by putting them into "B" shares, the ones that pay the broker the highest commissions. Although the characteristics of the class of shares differ from fund family to fund family, in general, "B" shares should be avoided. If an investor has to purchase load shares, he should consider A, C, or D shares. However, nontheless, all load shares should be avoided whenever possible.

Funds that have high turnover rates should also be avoided because high turnover rates cause an increase in trading costs; for long-term performance the lower the turnover, the better.

Except for some PIMCO bond funds, avoid funds that have turnover rates higher than 100%. PIMCO Total Return Bond Fund had a turnover rate of over 200% in 2003, but Bill Gross, who clearly knows what he is doing, guided it, so that's OK.

Choosing appropriate open-end mutual funds is no simple matter and takes a fair amount of research to look at the multitude of choices. Morningstar's Web site— **www.Morningstar. com** —can help you analyze mutual funds while also providing you with information with which to apply some of the statistical concepts discussed above. However, if you do not have the inclination or time, you can apply one of my simple investment models, using Exchange traded funds.

Appendix
Sources of Information

There are many sources of information available to the
investor, especially now that almost everyone has access to
the Internet. However, I am going to list the

sources of information and Web sites of
information that I believe are most important
to the intelligent investor. I have divided the
sources into groups for easier reference —
and, in some cases, I have provided the reader
with a brief description.

I am also providing a list of suggested reading materials as well as information on various institutions I feel will be valuable.

Suggested Readings

The Intelligent Investor — Written by the late Benjamin Graham
and updated by Jason Zweig. Warren Buffett said that in his
opinion, this was the best book on investing ever written. I tend
to agree with Mr. Buffett because *The Intelligent Investor,* which
has served me well over the years, is largely responsible for my
success.

Morningstar Guide to Mutual Funds — This is an excellent book
for mutual fund investors. Written in simple language, it is easy

to follow and understand; yet it is powerful and loaded with information that is invaluable to the fund investor.

The Morgan Stanley Dean Witter Guide to Personal Investing is an excellent primer for beginning investors. Written by a stockbroker, it has a slight bias towards stocks and full-service firms, but nonetheless, it is still quite useful.

Investing in REITs by Ralph Block is an excellent manual for those interested in purchasing REITs on the Exchanges; it contains and provides the reader with a wealth of valuable information.

The *Wall Street Journal* — The world's leading financial daily. A must-read for any serious investor.

Barrons—This sister publication of The Wall Street Journal is published every Monday and provides interesting articles, up-to-date economic news, and topics on a variety of investment themes. If you read one publication, this has to be it!

The Economist Magazine contains an excellent overview of business and economics and insightful articles about business and global affairs.

Web sites

www.morningstar.com — This site is packed with useful information for fund and ETF holders. Full description of ETF's closed-end funds and open-end funds are available.

www.amex.com — On the AMEX Web site, the investor can gather a significant amount of information about ETFs, including descriptions, holdings in the Exchange traded funds, and performance numbers.

www.nyse.com — The Web site of the New Stock Exchange

lists and describes the ETFs and closed-end funds traded on the "Big Board."

www.yahoo.com/finance — Yahoo Finance can give you quotes of ETF's closed- and open-end funds and charting capabilities. Performance numbers are also available.

www.bloomberg.com — Bloomberg is the largest and most important provider of financial information pertaining to bonds. This site provides the investor with a wealth of statistics, including yield to maturity, current yields, and current interest rates for all types of bonds, commercial paper, and money markets.

www.treasurydirect.gov — The U.S. Government's Web site that allows investors to purchase U.S. Treasuries and TIPS directly from the Federal Reserve without paying commission. The investor can establish an account with the Federal Reserve and the FED will hold all of the treasuries, TIPS, and Savings Bonds in custody. Why pay Fidelity or Schwab commissions when you can buy essentially the same thing at the FED for a lot less. **Everyone should have a Treasury Direct account.**

www.savingsbonds.gov — The U.S. Government's Web site that allows investors to purchase U.S. Savings Bonds Series I and Series EE. The investor can choose to have the Treasury Department mail the bond to the investor, or the Treasury can hold it in safekeeping for you — an excellent way to start saving, especially for the beginning investor.

www.fidelity.com — contains useful information for investors; and you can check your Fidelity account online, 24/7.

www.bcaresearch.com — site of one of the most respected economic and market consulting firms in North America.

www.iarfc.org — site to find interpretation of over 87 professional designations.

www.fp.edu — Web site of The College for Financial Planning, it also provides a good explanation of designations and is more concise than the Iarfc Website.

www.herzfeld.com — The site of the foremost authority on closed-end funds.

www.pimco.com — Web site of Pimco and home of the greatest bond manager alive, Bill Gross. Read his insightful and entertaining commentary.

www.stevensfirstprinciples.com — Web site that has useful information about investing and financial planning. Also has very useful portfolio tracker and financial planning calculators. Market and Mutual Fund quotes are part of this site as well.

Suggested Institutions

A note of caution: Because I am recommending the following institutions at the time of *this* writing, any of them may necessarily change and/or no longer be suitable. Therefore, you should consult a financial professional or investigate thoroughly before using any of the recommendations listed below.

Charles Schwab and Company Inc, nationwide offices — Excellent discount brokerage for trading and order execution. In my opinion, not suitable for investment advice.

Fidelity Investments, nationwide offices — Excellent discount brokerage for trading and order execution. In my opinion, not suitable for investment advice.

Fiduciary Trust International, Los Angeles and New York — Well respected trust company.

U.S. Trust Company — Well respected trust company.

Epilogue

Whew! We've covered a significant amount of material and I know there's much to absorb, but instead of trying to memorize or remember all of the information in this book, think of it as your desktop companion — a reference guide that you can open up and consult whenever necessary.

"Money is Freedom."

–Horace Walpole

Feel free to write in your book and underline the parts you really think are important. After all, it is *your* future, and you want to make it as comfortable as possible — unless, of course, you're imagining yourself working at some job you absolutely hate when you are old.

The only one you can depend on is you. The paternalistic politicians of our government are going to realize soon enough that they can no longer afford to pay for all the Social Security and Medicare benefits that they promised without greatly increasing taxes or cranking up the old government printing press.

Knowing the politicians, the least painful route for them is to inflate their way out of the mess they have caused but have refused to fix. Be prepared to expect less government benefits and possibly more taxes.

Regardless of how Social Security and Medicare are paid for, we can expect more inflation. Why? Because history has shown that inflation has averaged 4% or more over the past 75 years. Who knows exactly what the actual inflation rate will be since it is underestimated and the government calculates the inflation rate to their advantage? Even small amounts of inflation can create havoc in your retirement plans. So, now that you're aware of it, you'd better start to plan for it.

Since the government will not be able to take care of us, and inflation will continue, we need to save more and spend less. This simple fact, as uncomfortable as it may be for many of you, is unavoidable. The sooner you start to save, the better off you will be.

Saving starts with a personal balance sheet and income statement. You need to track what you spend and save 10% to 20% of your pretax wages. It might sound like a lot, but not doing it will ensure you a difficult retirement. If you save by paying yourself first and taking it off the top of your paycheck, you most likely will not even miss it. In fact, it's actually less painful to save this way. Once you know what you spend and start to save, you can construct a personal balance sheet. By using a financial calculator like the one located at **www.stevensfirstprinciples.com**, you can start to strategize different scenarios because you will know exactly what your asset base needs to be in order to pay for your retirement lifestyle.

Part of saving is not losing, and one of the best ways not to lose is to protect you. Your identity is precious, and you don't want anyone to steal your life away; so, of course, you will take precautions to make sure this does not happen to you.

Insurance in different forms is a cornerstone of smart protection, and you should get expert advice in this area. As a smart investor, you should not buy more insurance than you need, and you should save the money you don't spend on insurance for your retirement.

Contrary to popular belief, your attorney can be your friend, and you should consult one for a first-class estate plan.

What differentiates a successful person from an unsuccessful one is that the successful person seeks help when he either can't figure things out or doesn't have the time to do it himself.

The unsuccessful person doesn't have the wisdom to determine when he needs help and muddles through a difficult situation alone. Realize when you need help, and get it — but get help from the right advisor, not the wrong one.

Choose your counsel wisely, even if you have to pay for it, because in the long run, it will be worth it. The wrong counsel may put your retirement in jeopardy. Do business with reputable professionals who have a demonstrated track record of performance, safe handling of assets, and who give attention to their clients.

Check with the SEC or NASD to see if the advisor you want to use has any major violations. Avoid mass marketers and organizations that have armies of salesmen touting their services. Look for credentials such as CFA, CFP®, CMFC®, or CFS — at least they have a good knowledge of investments and have taken a rigorous examination to prove it. However, if you have the time and inclination to do it yourself, you will save a substantial amount of money in fees which, over time, will add up.

Remember: Investments are not static and need to be monitored from time-to-time. Your long-term goal is retirement. Therefore, you should have a long-term perspective and not get caught up in short-term market timing schemes touted by people who want to get their hands on your money.

When you get nervous about long-term investing, just think about working behind a cash register — that alone should set your mind at ease and make you want to stay the course. Fees and transaction costs are a drag on your portfolio and will reduce your long-term performance. High portfolio turnover causes unnecessary expenses and in taxable accounts, unnecessary taxes. John Bogle founded Vanguard Funds to keep expenses and turnover low. He was right; and you can be, too.

The best way to keep your long-term perspective in focus and keep transaction costs low is to use Exchange traded funds, rebalancing them only once a year. Some advisors charge a ridiculous fee to manage index funds, which is totally unnecessary. It's only satisfactory to pay a management fee of 1% to 1.25% for active management *if* you're getting results.

Make sure you ask for an advisor's performance record and that the performance timeframe is standardized. If you can't use Exchange traded funds, use closed or open-end funds, but use proper risk and evaluation measurement tools to be sure you are getting good value for your money.

Before you invest, you need to take inventory of yourself and figure out your investment psychology. Take the short quiz found in this book to determine what kind of investor you are. Don't go against your nature. If you're conservative, fine — then don't be aggressive with your investments.

By "crossing" your investment psychology, you will not be able to stick to your course of action when times get tough. If you don't stick to your investment plan, regardless of whether you're conservative or aggressive, your will end up without sufficient retirement funds.

I hope your journey is as enjoyable for you as it is for me — and I especially hope that this book can guide you along the way.